بسم الله الرّحمن الرّحيم

Title: The Integrity of the Family & the Role of Parents

ISBN: 978-1-952306-98-3

FIRST EDITION | MAY 2024

Author: HABIB UMAR BIN HAFIZ
Translator: ABDULLAH SALIH
Typesetting & Distribution: WWW.SATTAURPUBLISHING.COM

www.imamghazali.co

صَلاَحُ الأُسَرِةِ
وَدَوْرُ الأَبَوَيْنِ فِي التَّرْبِيَةِ

THE INTEGRITY OF THE
FAMILY & THE ROLE OF
PARENTS

◆ ◆ ◆

Habib Umar bin Hafiz

CONTENTS

—

THE AUTHOR

Habib Umar was born in Tarim, in Yemen's Hadramawt Valley. He is a direct descendant of the Messenger of Allah ﷺ through Imam al-Husayn. His father and his father's father and all his forefathers were scholars and knowers of Allah. Among his blessed forefathers are Imam Ali Zayn al-Abidin as well as the first of the Prophetic Household to settle in Hadramawt, Imam Ahmad bin Isa al-Muhajir and his noble descendants, al-Faqih al-Muqaddam Muhammad bin Ali, Shaykh Abd al-Rahman al-Saqqaf and Shaykh Abu Bakr bin Salim. His full lineage is as follows:

He is al-Habib al-Allamah Umar bin Muhammad bin Salim bin Hafiz bin Abdullah bin Abu Bakr bin Aydarus bin Umar bin Aydarus bin Umar bin Abu Bakr bin Aydarus bin al-Husayn bin al-Shaykh al-Fakhr Abu Bakr bin Salim bin Abdullah bin Abd al-Rahman bin Abdullah bin Shaykh Abd al-Rahman al-Saqqaf bin Shaykh Muhammad Mawla al-Dawilah, bin Ali Mawla al-Darak, bin Alawi al-Ghayur, bin al-Faqih al-Muqaddam Muhammad, bin Ali, bin Muhammad Sahib Mirbat, bin Ali Khali Qasam, bin Alawi, bin Muhammad Sahib al-Sawmaah, bin Alawi, bin Ubaydullah, bin al-Imam al-Muhajir il-Allah Ahmad, bin Isa, bin Muhammad al-Naqib, bin Ali al-Uraydi, bin Jafar al-Sadiq, bin Muhammad al-Baqir, bin Ali Zayn al-Abidin, bin Husayn al-Sibt, bin Ali bin Abi Talib and Fatimah al-Zahra', the daughter of our Master Muhammad, the Seal of the Prophets ﷺ.

HIS STUDY OF THE ISLAMIC SCIENCES

At an early age, Habib Umar memorized the Qur'an and began studying the Islamic sciences under his father and many of the great scholars of Tarim of the time. Among them were Habib Muhammad bin Alawi bin Shihab, Habib Ahmad bin Ali Ibn Shaykh Abu Bakr, Habib Abdullah bin Shaykh al-Aydarus, Habib Abdullah bin Hasan Balfaqih, Habib Umar bin Alawi al-Kaf, Habib Ahmad bin Hasan al-Haddad, Habib Hasan bin Abdullah al-Shatiri and his brother, Habib Salim, the Mufti, Shaykh Fadl bin Abd al-Rahman Ba Fadl, and Shaykh Tawfiq Aman. He also studied under his older brother, Habib Ali al-Mashhur, who was the Mufti of Tarim.

HIS MIGRATION TO AL-BAYDA'

In 1387 (1967), a socialist government came to power in South Yemen which attempted to eradicate Islam from society. Scholars were persecuted and religious institutions were forcibly closed. In spite of this, Habib Umar's father, Habib Muhammad, fearlessly continued calling people to Allah. He was required to register with the security forces on a regular basis so that they could check on his whereabouts. Thus, on Friday morning on 29th Dhu'l-Hijjah 1392 (1973) he left Habib Umar, then only nine years of age, in the mosque before the Friday prayer and went to register. He was never seen again. Habib Umar remained in Tarim under the care of his blessed mother, Hababah Zahra bint Hafiz al-Haddar and his older brother, Habib Ali al-Mashhur. The situation in Hadramawt became increasingly difficult and thus in Safar 1402 (1981), Habib Umar migrated to the city of al-Bayda' in North Yemen, safe from the socialist regime in South Yemen.

He resided in the Ribat of al-Bayda' and studied at the hands of the founder of the Ribat, the great Imam, Habib Muhammad bin Abdullah al-Haddar, as well as Habib Zayn bin Ibrahim bin Sumayt, the Ribat's main teacher. Habib Muhammad held him in high regard and could see the future that was awaiting him. He duly married his daughter to him. Habib Umar inherited his father's passion for teaching people and calling them to Allah ﷻ, and he had begun this noble work at the age of fifteen, but it was in al-Bayda that he had the opportunity to work freely. He had a great impact on the youth of the city and was a means for many of them to become students in the Ribat and then scholars and callers to Allah ﷻ. He established a number of weekly lessons and gatherings of knowledge. He would often travel in order to call to Allah ﷻ in the area around of al-Bayda', just as he would travel further afield to al-Hudaydah and Ta'izz. He used to frequently visit Ta'izz in order to take knowledge from the great scholar, Habib Ibrahim bin Aqil bin Yahya.

HIS REPEATED VISITS TO THE HIJAZ

During his time in al-Bayda', Habib Umar made frequent visits to the Hijaz. There he learnt from the great Imams of the time: Habib Abd al-Qadir al-Saqqaf, Habib Ahmad Mashhur al-Haddad, and Habib Abu Bakr al-Attas al-Habashi. He took license to narrate from the chains of transmission in Hadith and in other sciences from Shaykh Muhammad Yasin al-Faddani and the Hadith scholar of the Two Sanctuaries, Sayyid Muhammad bin Alawi al-Maliki, as well as other scholars.

HIS MOVE TO OMAN AND AL-SHIHR

After the fall of the socialist regime in 1410 (1990) and the unification of North and South Yemen, Habib Umar returned to Hadramawt. He visited Tarim, and then settled with some of his students in city of Salalah in the Sultanate of Oman. For a year and a half he called people to Allah in the region and then in 1413 (1992) he moved to the city of al-Shihr, which lies on the Indian Ocean in the province of Hadramawt. The Ribat of al-Mustafa had recently been reopened after closure during the days of the socialist regime. Habib Umar began teaching in the Ribat and reviving its traditions. Many students from different regions of Yemen and parts of South-East Asia came to seek knowledge from him.

HIS RETURN TO TARIM

Habib Umar then returned to his home city and immediately began to breathe new life into the religious life of the region. His tireless work led to the establishment of Dar al-Mustafa in 1414 (1994). Dar al-Mustafa is a centre for traditional Islamic learning based upon three foundations: the first is ilm (knowledge), learning the sciences of the Sacred Law from those who are qualified to impart them through connected chains of transmission; the second is tazkiyah, purifying the soul and refining one's character and the third is dawah, calling to Allah and conveying beneficial knowledge. Dar al-Mustafa began in Habib Umar's house next to the Mawla Aidid mosque and a batch of students from South East Asia came to study with him, as well as students from Tarim and other parts of Yemen. As the number of students increased, the need for a purpose-built building became clear. Land was duly purchased and building started. Dar al-Mustafa was officially opened in 1417 (1997). Habib Umar honored his father's sacrifice by making the opening date 29th

Dhu'l-Hijjah, the day on which Habib Muhammad was abducted. Although Dar al-Mustafa was established recently, it is intimately connected to the illustrious legacy of the scholarly tradition of Hadramawt, which stretches back more than a thousand years. In this we witness the renewal of the religion (tajdid) that is taking place at the hands of Habib Umar.

Dar al-Zahra' was opened in 1422 (2001) to provide learning opportunities for women as well. A number of branches of Dar al-Mustafa have since been opened in Hadramawt and South East Asia. A branch has been opened in the Yemeni capital, Sana', and older ribats have also been revived, such as the ribats of al-Shihr, Mukalla' and Aynat. Dar al-Mustafa and its branches continue to grow and receive students from all corners of the earth.

HIS TRAVELS

Habib Umar constantly travels to convey the Prophetic message and to call people to Allah. He delivers regular lectures and khutbahs within Hadramawt and often makes trips abroad. His travels have taken him to almost all the Arab states, East and South Africa, South East Asia and Australia, the Indian Subcontinent, Western Europe and Scandinavia and North America. He has connected to the chains of transmission of the scholars of these regions and has also participated in many Islamic conferences.

HIS WRITINGS AND PUBLICATIONS

Although Habib Umar is best known for his speeches and lessons, he has authored several works. Among them are al-Dhakirah al-Musharrafah, which contains personally obligatory knowledge for every Muslim, and three short hadith compilations, Mukhtar al-Hadith, Nur al-Iman and Qutuf al-Falihin. His Qabas al-Nur al-Mubin is a summarised version of the third quarter of Imam al-Ghazali's Ihya' Ulum al-Din and is an expression of his concern for curing the ailments of the heart. It also reflects the love and respect that the Ba Alawi scholars have traditionally had for Ihya' Ulum al-Din. A selection of Habib Umar's speeches and wisdoms have been collected in Tawjihat al-Tullab and Tawjih al-Nabih, and some of his khutbahs have been collected in Fayd al-Imdad. Khulasat al-Madad al-Nabawi is Habib Umar's compilation of adhkar for the seeker to recite on a daily basis. It contains Prophetic invocations and the litanies of many of the great Imams. His mawlid compositions, al-Diya' al-La-mi' and al-Sharab al-Tahur are recited in gatherings throughout the world, as are his poems.

THE INTEGRITY OF THE FAMILY & THE ROLE OF PARENTS

◆ ◆ ◆

Habib Umar bin Hafiz

صَلَاحُ الأُسَرَةِ
وَدَوَرُ الأَبَوَينِ فِي التَّرْبِيَةِ

...

للعلامة المربي الحبيب

عُمَرُ بنُ مُحَمَّدِ بنِ سَالِمِ بنِ حَفِيظٍ

ابنُ الشَّيخِ أبي بَكرِ بنِ سَالِمٍ

Introduction

All praise is due to Allah ﷻ. Prayers and peace be upon the most honourable of prophets and messengers, our Master Muhammad, the truthful and trustworthy; upon his pleasant and pure household; his rightly guided and guiding companions; and those who follow them upon beneficence until Judgment Day.

To proceed: The responsibility related to the righteousness of the family and the rearing of children is from among the greatest responsibilities which the father and mother mutually play a part in, which is related to the parental obligations in the rearing of children, and the establishment of perception and understanding of Allah ﷻ. In fact, His *System of Successorship* upon His land through a family which is supported and assisted by a school system, where boys and girls receive a portion of information related to the Noble Revelation; religious jurisprudence; honorable Prophetic way; etiquettes of the Chosen one, the father of Al-Zahra (abundant peace and blessings be upon him, his household, and companions); in addition to other sciences from different subjects, they become prepared to establish a role from among the roles of Allah's ﷻ *System of Successorship* upon His land.

المقدمة

الحمد لله رب العالمين، والصلاة والسلام على أشرف الأنبياء والمرسلين، سيدنا محمد الصادق الأمين، وعلى آله الطيبين الطاهرين، وأصحابه الهداة المهتدين، والتابعين لهم بإحسان إلى يوم الدين.

وبعد: فإن مهمة صلاح الأسرة وتربية الأبناء من أعظم المهمات التي يشترك في القيام بها الأب والأم، وهي مهمة تتعلق بشأن واجب الأبوين في التربية، وإقامة أسس الوعي والفهم عن الله، بل وأسس الخلافة عنه تعالى في أرضه عبر الأسرة، وتأتي المدرسة مساندةً ومساعدةً لها، حيث يتلقَّى الأبناء والبنات فيها نصيباً من أخبار الوحي الكريم، والفقه في الدين العظيم، والسنة الغرّاء، وآداب المصطفى أبي الزهراء صلى الله عليه وآله وصحبه وسلم، مع ما يتلقون من معلومات أخرى في مختلف المواد وبذلك يتهيَّؤُون للقيام بدورٍ من أدوار الخلافة عن الله تعالى في أرضه.

Understanding of the
System of Successorship

The meaning of Allah's ﷻ *System of Successorship* upon His land:

The Establishment of His satisfactory Way was through that which He explained in what was revealed to His Prophet, the Chosen one, Muhammad ﷺ. He ended through him Prophethood and Messengership and made him the Master of the people of Qur'ān and Guidance ﷺ. Therefore, indeed every act, path, and movement in life which contradicts this Divine Way is the cause of the corruption of mankind, his condition, community, life, and Hereafter. So, no corruption, nor evil, nor a deviation from joy and blessing for a person occurs except by opposing the Way of Allah ﷻ in speech, act, and intention.

So, carrying out that which is beloved to Allah ﷻ in speech, actions, and intentions is what is meant by Allah's ﷻ *System of Successorship* upon His land and this structure is made complete in families, homes, and communities, through various worldly affairs, such as professions, trades, and other different work. Beneficence of a worker toward his work in his profession, trade, farming, teaching, employment, manufacturing, sewing and the likes, should be together with carrying out the primary role which is that role related to his family and home. He should be fulfilling his obligation in his house with mercy, love, and a realization that we are slaves of a God who did not create us in vain nor for play. Our Lord says: {{Did you think that We had created you in vain and that you were not to re-

مفهوم الخلافة

معنى الخلافة عن الله تعالى في أرضه: إقامةُ منهاجِه الذي ارتضاه وبيَّنَه في ما أوحاه إلى نبيه المصطفى محمد ﷺ، الذي ختم به النبوة والرسالة، وجعله سيد أهل البيان والدلالة ﷺ.

وذلك أن كلَّ عمل، وكلَّ مسار، وكلَّ حركةٍ في الحياة تخالفُ هذا المنهج الإلهي هي سببُ فساد الإنسان وفساد حاله ومجتمعه ودنياه وآخرته. فلا يحصل فساد ولا شر ولا خروج عن الحبور والحيور للإنسان إلا بمخالفته لمنهج الله تعالى في قولٍ وفعلٍ ونيةٍ.

فالقيام على ما يحبُّ الله في الأفعال والنيات والأقوال هو الخلافة عن الله تبارك وتعالى في أرضه، تتمُّ به العمارة للأسر والديار والمجتمعات بمختلف شؤون حياتها .. في المِهن والحِرف والأعمال المختلفة، ويكون إحسانُ العامل لعمله في مهنته، وفي حِرفته، وفي زراعته، وفي تدريسه، وفي وظيفته، وفي صناعته، وفي خياطته.. إلى غير ذلك، مع القيام بالدور الأصيل، وهو دوره في الأسرة، ودوره في البيت، وذلك بقيام الإنسان بواجبه في بيته على أساس الرحمة والألفة، وإدراك أننا عبيدٌ لإلهٍ خلقنا لا عبثاً ولا لعباً، يقول ربنا:

turn to Us. So exalted is Allah, the Sovereign, the Truth...}} Surah
Al-Muminuun, verses 115-116.

﴿أَفَحَسِبْتُمْ أَنَّمَا خَلَقْنَاكُمْ عَبَثًا وَأَنَّكُمْ إِلَيْنَا لَا تُرْجَعُونَ. فَتَعَالَى اللهُ الْمَلِكُ
الْحَقُّ﴾ [المؤمنون: ١١٥-١١٦] من هذا العبث.

Rearing from a Divine Perspective

Rearing is the preservation, practice, and execution of the Divine Commands in reality to paint the souls with the color of magnification toward these commands and a desire for their implementation.

Initial manifestations of rearing during the era of Prophecy:

Indeed, the responsibility of rearing, since the Master of rearers first carried it was cast into the chest and heart of a pious woman Khadija, daughter of Khuwaylid (May Allah be pleased with her), so she is the first to know about this affair of rearing and the secret of this Message and Sacred Law. Since the moment that Allah ﷻ revealed upon him when he was in the cave, he ﷺ went to the house of Khadija (May Allah be pleased with her) and cast toward her this trust and Message and thereafter, glad tidings and joy descended upon her heart, by the blessing of the Protector. Thus, she began attending to her soul in a tranquil way until faith firmly became established in her heart, causing her to arrive at the degrees of certainty in Him. She then played a great part at the outset of the *Da'wah*, by subjugating herself to this Message, her intellect, cogitation, soul, broad reputation, and abundant wealth, sacrificing all of that in path of giving victory to Allah ﷻ and His Messenger, the chosen Prophet, Muhammad ﷺ, to the extent that the Hadiths have informed us about Allah's honoring of her. She came to the Prophet ﷺ carrying a bowl of food and thereafter placed it before the Prophet ﷺ, who

التربية من منظور رباني

مفهوم التربية هو القيام على حراسة الأوامر الإلهية وتطبيقها وتنفيذها في الواقع، وصبغ النفوس بصبغة الإعظام لهذه الأوامر والرغبة في العمل بها.

أول مظاهر التربية من عهد النبوة:

إن مهمة التربية منذ أن حملها سيد المربين ﷺ في أول ما حملها ألقاها إلى صدر وقلب المرأة الصالحة.. خديجة بنت خويلد، فهي أول مَن عرف خبر هذه التربية وسر هذه الرسالة والشريعة؛ فأول ما أوحى الله إليه وهو في الغار خرج إلى بيت خديجة ﵂ فألقى عليها هذه الأمانة وهذه الرسالة، فنازل قلبَها البشرى والفرح بنعمة المولى، وأخذت تعالجُ نفسَها في طمأنينة حتى تَمَكَّنَ الإيمان من قلبها فأوصلها إلى مراتب اليقين به، فقامت بعظيم الدور من بداية الدعوة، وسخّرت لهذه الرسالة عقلَها وفكرها ونفسها وجاهَها الواسع ومالَها الكثير، وبذلت كلَّ ذلك في سبيل نصرة الله ورسوله النبي المصطفى محمد ﷺ، حتى حمل لنا الحديثُ تكريمَ الله لها وقد دخلت على النبي ﷺ حاملةً إناءً فيه طعامٌ فوضعته بين يديه فقال لها الرسول ﷺ يا خديجة هذا جبريل يقول: «هَذِهِ خَدِيجَةُ قَدْ أَتَتْ مَعَهَا إِنَاءٌ فِيهِ إِدَامٌ، أَوْ طَعَامٌ أَوْ شَرَابٌ، فَإِذَا هِيَ أَتَتْكَ فَاقْرَأْ عَلَيْهَا السَّلَامَ مِنْ رَبِّهَا وَمِنِّي وَبَشِّرْهَا

then said: "O Khadijah, Angel Gabriel said: 'Khadijah will come with a bowl of stew, food or drink, so when she comes to you, convey greetings of peace to her on behalf of her Lord and on my behalf and give her glad tidings of a house in Paradise, in which there is no noise nor tiredness, made of jewelry.'"[1]

So Khadijah (May Allah be pleased with her) responded by saying: "Allah is peace, the source and destination of peace, and upon Angel Gabriel be Allah's peace, mercy, and blessing."

{{"Peace", a word from a Merciful Lord.}} Surah Yasin, verse 58.

He ﷺ spoke about this role which she played to our Liegelady and Mother of the believers, Aisha (May Allah be pleased with her), who saw his honor and courtesy toward her, to the extent that whenever he slaughtered a sheep, he would divide it among the friends of Khadijah (May Allah be pleased with her) saying: "So and so visited us during the time of Khadijah, so show her generosity."[2] So the Liegelady Aisha (May Allah be pleased with her) would say: "What makes you remember an old woman from among the old women of Quraysh, when Allah ﷻ has replaced her with someone better?"[3]

So the Messenger and rearer ﷺ turned to her and reared her and prepared Aisha as a result of that and said to her: "No, by Allah, He ﷻ has not replaced her with someone better, she had faith in me when the people had no faith in me, she believed in me when the people disbelieved in me, she accommodated me when the people pushed me away and she sacrificed herself and wealth for me, so by

1 Narrated by Al-Bukhari, on the authority of Abu Hurayrah, Chapter of Marriage of the Prophet ﷺ, Dar Tawq al-Najaah, 1st Ed. / 1422 AH.

2 Transmitted by Al-Haakim in Al-Mustadrak from the narrations of Aisha (1/62/40) Dar Ul Kutub Al 'Ilmiyyah–Beirut, 1st Ed. 1990–1411 and he said: "This is a sound Hadith, according to the conditions of Imam al-Bukhari and Muslim, who were both in agreement about its narration being utilized as a proof in many Hadiths, without there being a defect.

3 Transmitted by Al-Bukhari, on the authority of Aisha (May Allah be pleased with her), Chapter of Marriage of the Prophet ﷺ, (3821/39/5), Dar Tawq al-Najaah, 1st Ed. / 1422 AH.

بِبَيْتٍ فِي الْجَنَّةِ مِنْ قَصَبٍ - أي لؤلؤ مجوف - لاَ صَخَبَ فِيهِ، وَلاَ نَصَبَ » [١]
فقالت خديجة: (الله السلام ومنه السلام وإليه يعود السلام وعلى جبريل
السلام ورحمة الله وبركاته) رضي الله عنها وأرضاها ﴿سَلَامٌ قَوْلًا مِّن رَّبٍّ رَّحِيمٍ﴾
[يس: ٥٨]

ولقد عَبَّرَ ﷺ عن هذا الدور الذي قامت به فقال لسيدتنا أم المؤمنين
عائشة رضي الله عنها حينما رأت إكرامه لخديجة وحفظه للمعروف، إذ كان يذبح
الشاة فيقسمها في صويحبات خديجة ويقول: «إن فلانة كانت تأتينا أيام
خديجة فأكرموه»[٢] فكانت السيدة عائشة تقول: (ما تذكُرُ مِن عجوز من
عجائز قريش قد أبدلك الله خيرًا منها)[٣]. فالتفت إليها رسول الله المربي وربها
وهَيَّأ عائشة بذلك للتربية، فقال لها: «لا والله ما أبدلني الله خيرًا منها، لقد
آمنت بي حين كفر الناس، وصدقتني حين كذبني الناس وآوتني حين طردني
الناس، وفدتني بنفسها ومالها، فلا والله ما أبدلني الله خيرًا منها»[٤] فتَرَبَّتْ
عائشة على حفظ المعروف وذكر الفضل لأهله، متجاوزة في ذلك العواطف
واعتبارات الصغر والكبر من عجوزٍ وشابةٍ، ومن ثيب وبكرٍ، بل تجاوزت كل
هذه الاعتبارات لأجل إقامة ميزان الإكرام لأهل البذل في سبيل الله تبارك وتعالى
وأهل التضحية وأهل العطاء، فهو ميزان الكرامة والشرف والعز والسيادة،

١   رواه البخاري عن أبي هريرة، باب تزويج النبي ﷺ (٣٨٢٠/٣٩/٥) دار طوق النجاة، ط ١ / ١٤٢٢هـ.

٢   أخرجه الحاكم في المستدرك من حديث عائشة، (٤٠/٦٢/١) دار الكتب العلمية - بيروت - ط ١ - ١٤١١ - ١٩٩٠
وقال: هذا حديث صحيح على شرط الشيخين فقد اتفقا على الاحتجاج برواته في أحاديث كثيرة وليس له علة.

٣   أخرجه البخاري عن عائشة، باب تزويج النبي ﷺ (٣٨٢١/٣٩/٥) دار طوق النجاة، ط ١ / ١٤٢٢هـ

٤   أخرجه أحمد في مسنده، مسند الصديقة عائشة رضي الله عنها (٢٤٨٦٤/٣٥٦/٤١) مؤسسة الرسالة ط ١ / ١٤٢١هـ

Allah, He ﷻ has not replaced her with someone better."[4] So Aisha (May Allah be pleased with her) was reared toward the preservation of courtesy and remembrance of the merit of his family, paying no attention to feelings or considerations of youth or old age, be it an old or young woman, non-virgin or virgin. In fact, she disregarded all these considerations in order to establish the measure of honor toward those who give in the path of Allah ﷻ, the people of sacrifice and charity, which is the scale of generosity, honor, pride, and Mastership which Aisha (May Allah be pleased with her) learned. She began making mention of this conversation between her and the Messenger ﷺ, conveying it to the Nation and accurately implementing it, disregarding her inner and outer nature and the human inclination toward authority and being honored, praised, and appreciated. She would then prefer the praise and appreciation of the previous wife of the Chosen one, Muhammad ﷺ, which is a sign from among the signs of this great rearing.

---

4 Transmitted by Ahmad in his Musnad.

تعلمت ذلك عائشة، فأخذت تذكر هذا الحديث الجاري بينها وبين رسول الله
وتبلغه للأمة، وتؤديه كما هو، تتجاوز في ذلك نفسيتها وبشريتها وإرادة الإنسان
أن يكون هو صاحب المكانة وأن يكون هو المكرَم، ومِن أن يؤثر عنه المدح
والثناء، وهي تؤثر المدح والثناء لضرتها الزوجة السابقة للمصطفى محمد،
وهذا أثرٌ مِن آثار هذه التربية العظيمة.

Influencing Factors of Rearing

The responsibility of Allah's 🕮 *System of Successorship* is related to your everyday life; that which revolves within your homes and in particular that which is connected to your sons and daughters, so these connections, actions, everyday occurrences, and that which emanates from your speech and actions has an enormous effect toward a good or bad direction and consistency or inconsistency upon the path of Allah 🕮. This is because we are up against influencing and transformative agents in life and various promptings having an effect on our youth and elders.

If our reins, especially those of fathers and mothers, are not fastened to truth, the Prophet of Truth 🕮, and that which he conveyed from Allah 🕮, influencing factors will invade our minds, intentions, objectives, deeds, and outlook on life, and thereafter have an effect on us until we become deviated.

If a deviation occurs, this results in a drifting behind evil, mischief, and malicious acts to the point where the family lives some aspects of life, as a life of the disbelievers, evil doers, sinners, and a life of one who does not believe in the Messenger of Allah and Beloved of the Creator, Muhammad 🕮.

All this is from the effects of the negative agents governing the family in its course of life, in a state of heedlessness and not surrendering its reins to the Truth 🕮 and the best of creation, Muhammad 🕮. In accordance to what our Lord has mentioned regarding the way He decrees and rules over us through Sacred Laws: {{It is not

عوامل التأثير في التربية

المهمة في هذه الخلافة عن الله تعالى تتعلق بيومياتكم، وما يجري في دياركم، وخصوصاً فيما يتعلق بالأبناء والبنات، فهذه الصلات والأعمال واليوميات وما يصدر منكم من أقوال وأفعال له التأثيرُ الكبيرُ على حُسنِ المسيرِ أو سوئه، وعلى الاستقامة على منهج الله أو المخالفة له، لأننا أمام مؤثراتٍ ومتغيراتٍ في الحياة، ودواعٍ مختلفات تؤثر على صغارنا وكبارنا.

فإذا لم يكن زمانُنا - خصوصاً الآباء والأمهات - مزموماً بالإتباع للحق ولرسول الحق محمد ﷺ في ما جاء به عن الله تعالى، تدخَّلت المؤثراتُ علينا في فكرِنا و نياتنا و مقاصدنا و أعمالنا ونظرتنا للحياة، فأثَّرتْ علينا فانحرفنا.

وإذا حصل الانحرافُ جاء الانحرافُ وراء المساوئ والشرور والآفات والمفسدات، حتى ربما عاشت الأسرة في بعض نواحي حياتها عيشةَ الكفار والأشرار والفساق، وعيشةَ مَن لا يؤمن برسول الله محمد حبيبِ الخلاق صلى الله عليه وآله وصحبه وسلم.

fitting for a believing man nor woman, when Allah and His Messenger have decided a matter, that they should have any choice in their matter and whoever disobeys Allah and His Messenger, has certainly strayed into clear error.}} Surah Al-Ahzab, verse 36.

That which Allah ﷻ has given mankind, in terms of freedom and choice, is in that which He ﷻ has deemed permissible but not that which He ﷻ and the Messenger ﷺ have ruled against, so as for that which He ﷻ and the Messenger ﷺ have deemed obligatory and impermissible, no choice exists therein for anyone, nor is it befitting for a believing man and woman, regardless of the time or location to have a say in their matter.

He ﷻ says: {{… and when they are called to [the words of] Allah and His Messenger, to judge between them, at once a party of them turns aside [in refusal], but if the right is theirs, they come to him in prompt obedience. Is there a disease in their hearts, or have they doubted, or do they fear that Allah will be unjust to them or His Messenger? Rather, it is they who are the wrongdoers.}} Surah Al-Nur, verses 48-50. Refuge is in Allah ﷻ.

He ﷻ says: {{But no, by your Lord, they will not [truly] believe until they make you [O Muhammad] judge concerning that over which they dispute among themselves and then find within themselves no discomfort from what you have judged and submit completely.}} Surah Al-Nisa, verse 65.

كلُّ هذا مِن تأثير العوامل السلبية على الأسرة في حياتها مع غفلتها وعدم تسليمها الزِّمام للحق وخير الأنام محمد ﷺ، الذي قال ربنا فيما يقضي وفيما يحكم بيننا مِن أحكام: ﴿ وَمَا كَانَ لِمُؤْمِنٍ وَلَا مُؤْمِنَةٍ إِذَا قَضَى اللهُ وَرَسُولُهُ أَمْرًا أَن يَكُونَ لَهُمُ الْخِيَرَةُ مِنْ أَمْرِهِمْ وَمَن يَعْصِ اللهَ وَرَسُولَهُ فَقَدْ ضَلَّ ضَلَالًا مُّبِينًا ﴾ [الأحزاب: ٣٦].

فما أعطى اللهُ الإنسانَ مِن حريةٍ واختيارٍ فهو في ما أباح له في غير ما قضى سبحانه وتعالى وقضى رسولُه، أما ما أوجب اللهُ وأوجب رسولُه، وحرَّم اللهُ وحرَّم رسولُه فليس لأحد اختيار فيه، وليس لمؤمنٍ ولا مؤمنة في أيِّ زمان ولا في أيِّ مكان أن تكون لهم الْخِيَرَةُ مِن أمرهم قَطُّ.

يقول ﷻ ﴿ وَإِذَا دُعُوا إِلَى اللهِ وَرَسُولِهِ لِيَحْكُمَ بَيْنَهُمْ إِذَا فَرِيقٌ مِّنْهُم مُّعْرِضُونَ. وَإِن يَكُن لَّهُمُ الْحَقُّ يَأْتُوا إِلَيْهِ مُذْعِنِينَ. أَفِي قُلُوبِهِم مَّرَضٌ أَمِ ارْتَابُوا أَمْ يَخَافُونَ أَن يَحِيفَ اللهُ عَلَيْهِمْ وَرَسُولُهُ بَلْ أُولَٰئِكَ هُمُ الظَّالِمُونَ ﴾ [النور: ٤٨ - ٥٠] والعياذ بالله ﷻ. ويقول ﷻ: ﴿ فَلَا وَرَبِّكَ لَا يُؤْمِنُونَ حَتَّىٰ يُحَكِّمُوكَ فِيمَا شَجَرَ بَيْنَهُمْ ثُمَّ لَا يَجِدُوا فِي أَنفُسِهِمْ حَرَجًا مِّمَّا قَضَيْتَ وَيُسَلِّمُوا تَسْلِيمًا ﴾ [النساء: ٦٥

Role of a Woman

Men are usually outdoors, occupied with a variety of created objects, such as wood, stone, cement, iron, the ocean, vehicles, ships, trees, and plants, but the role of a woman at home is not to rectify any of these different created objects, except the most superior type of creation—a human being. So, she does not occupy herself with plants nor animals nor inanimate objects, as she has been tasked with a lofty task, since Allah ﷻ has made her occupation with the master of all types of creation, making her primary role the taking care of the human being, so how honorable is this role! How great is this duty! So, she is the one who assumes the responsibility of rearing from the outset.

وظيفة المرأة

يتعامل الرجال خارج المنازل غالباً مع أجناس الوجود؛ هذا مع الخشب وهذا مع الحجارة وهذا مع الإسمنت وهذا مع الحديد، وهذا مع البحر وهذا مع السيارات، وهذا مع السفن وهذا مع الأشجار والنبات، لكن المرأة دورها في البيت لا لِتُصْلِحَ شيئاً من الأجناس العادية ولكن مع أعلى أجناس الوجودِ وهو الإنسان؛ فهي لا تتعامل مع مستوى نباتٍ ولا حيوانٍ ولا جمادٍ، فقد أُوكلت إليها مهمةٌ ساميةٌ؛ إذ جعل الله شغلها مع سيِّد الأجناس، فكان دورُ المرأة الأساسي عنايتها بالإنسان نفسه، فما أكرم هذا الدور! وما أعظم هذه المهمة! فهي التي تتولى التربية من البداية.

Company and its Effects on Rearing

The effects of company are very significant; the Messenger of Allah ﷺ said: "A man follows the religion of his friend…"[5]

Company can be gained through various means—watching videos, various television channels, and reading. All company has a reflecting and influencing effect; every goodness has its effect. Likewise, that with which we watch and listen, is there another door to the heart, except the eye and ear? Regarding these two, the Compeller said: {{The hearing, sight and heart, of each of those, you will be questioned [by Allah]}} Surah Al-Isra, verse 36. So, the hearing and sight have a strong connection with the heart, as they are the two doors which bring to the heart that which reaches them. How many a word was the reason of permanent misguidance, how many a sight was the reason of a turning away from the path of Allah ﷻ until death, how many a sight or that which was listened to was the reason for turning towards Allah ﷻ—a change of state from bad to good? So, it is mandatory to pay attention to the doors of the heart—the ears and eyes, and to be aware of rearing in accordance to these Divine directives: {{Say to the believing men that they should lower their gaze and guard their modesty. That is purer and best for them. Surely, Allah is well acquainted with what that they do and say to the believing women that they should lower their gaze and guard their modesty.}} Surah Al-Nur, verses 30-31.

---

5   Transmitted by Ahmad on the authority of Abu Hurayrah, chapter of Musnad of Abu Hurayrah (8028/398/13) Muasistah al-Risalah, 1ˢᵗ Ed / 1421AH.

المجالسة وأثرها في التربية

تأثير المجالسة كبيرٌ جدًّا، قال رسول الله ﷺ «المرء على دين خليله»[5]. وتحصل المجالسات الآن بالوسائل المختلفة؛ فمنها المجالسات بأشرطة الفيديو، والمجالسات بالكتب والمجالسات بشاشات التلفزيون بمختلف القنوات، كلها مجالسات لها انعكاسات ولها تأثيرات بلا مغالطة عند العاقل المؤمن، فلكلِّ خيرٍ تأثيرُه، ولكلِّ شرٍّ يُشاهَد أو يُسمَع تأثيرُه أيضًا، وهل للقلب من باب إلا السمع والبصر! وعنهما قال الجبار ﴿إِنَّ السَّمْعَ وَالْبَصَرَ وَالْفُؤَادَ كُلُّ أُولَئِكَ كَانَ عَنْهُ مَسْئُولًا﴾ [الإسراء: ٣٦] فالسمع والبصر عظيما الارتباط بالفؤاد؛ إذ هما بابان يوصل إلى الفؤاد ما وصل إليهما؛ فما وصل إلى السمع والبصر نازل الفؤاد؛ فكم من كلمة كانت سبب إغواء إلى الأبد، وكم من منظر كان سبب رجوع عَن طريق الله إلى الموت، وكم من منظور أو مسموع كان سببًا للإقبال على الله وتغيير الحال من سوءٍ إلى حسن، فوجب الاعتناء بباب القلب: السمع والبصر؛ ووجب الانتباه في القيام بالتربية على ضوء هذه التوجيهات الإلهية ﴿قُل لِّلْمُؤْمِنِينَ يَغُضُّوا مِنْ أَبْصَارِهِمْ وَيَحْفَظُوا فُرُوجَهُمْ ذَلِكَ أَزْكَى لَهُمْ إِنَّ اللهَ خَبِيرٌ بِمَا يَصْنَعُونَ. وَقُل لِّلْمُؤْمِنَاتِ يَغْضُضْنَ مِنْ أَبْصَارِهِنَّ وَيَحْفَظْنَ فُرُوجَهُنَّ﴾ [النور: ٣٠ - ٣١]

---

٥ أخرجه أحمد عن أبي هريرة : باب مسند أبي هريرة (١٣ / ٣٩٨ / ٨٠٢٨) مؤسسة الرسالة ط ١٤٢١/١هـ

Marriage and Rearing

If a woman marries, her role in rearing becomes significant. Despite the fact that men are the maintainers of women, women however, have an effect in the straightening out of the men in terms of the execution of the right of maintenance and walking upright. The opposite significantly applies, in terms of their role.

So, when the natural of thought of marriage flows into the heart and mind, directives follow: What is the purpose of marriage? What is the intention for marriage? What is the wisdom for marriage? What is the effect of marriage?

In order for a woman and man to receive the role of rearing from the beginning it is upon them to understand their roles:

The role of the woman: "If someone whose religion and character you are pleased with, approaches you, then marry (her to) him." [6]

The role of the family: "...select the one who is religiously-committed and you will prosper."[7]

The role of the man and his family: {{If you don't do so, there will be discord in the land and great corruption.}} Surah Al-Anfaal, verse 73.

---

6 Transmitted by Ibn Majah in his book *Sunan*, on the authority of Abu Hurayrah, chapter of compatibility (1968/633/1) Publisher: Dar Ihyaa kutubul Arabiyya–Faysal Eesa, Al-Baabi Al-Halabi.

7 Transmitted by Al-Bukhari in his book *Sahih*, on the authority of Abu Hurayrah, chapter of compatibility in religion. (5090/7/7), Dar Tawq al-Najaah, 1ˢᵗ Ed. / 1422 AH.

الزواج والتربية

تتزوج المرأة فيكون لها الدور الكبير في التربية، ومع أن الرجال قوامون على النساء؛ فالنساء لهن تأثير في اعتدال الرجال وأداءُ حقِّ القوامة والمشي على الاستقامة، وفي عكس ذلك لهن الدور الكبير أيضا. فحينما يسري التفكير بحكم الطبع والبشرية في القلب والعقل في التزوج؛ تأتي التوجيهات، ما المقصود من الزواج ؟ وما النية عند الزواج ؟! وما الحكمة في الزواج ؟! وما النتيجة من الزواج ؟! ولتستلم المرأة ويستلم الرجل دور التربية من البداية عليهم أن يفقهوا أدوارهم:

فدور المرأة: «إذا أتاكم من ترضون دينه وخلقه فزوجوه» ٦. ودور الأسرة: «فاظفر بذات الدين تربت يداك» ٧.

ودور الزوج وأسرته ﴿إِلَّا تَفْعَلُوهُ تَكُنْ فِتْنَةٌ فِي الْأَرْضِ وَفَسَادٌ كَبِيرٌ﴾ [الأنفال: ٧٣]

---

٦ أخرجه ابن ماجه في سننه عن أبي هريرة ، باب الأكفاء (١/ ٦٣٢/ ١٩٦٧) لناشر : دار إحياء الكتب العربية - فيصل عيسى البابي الحلبي

٧ أخرجه البخاري في صحيحه عن أبي هريرة ، باب الأكفاء في الدين (٥٠٩٠/٧/٧) دار طوق النجاة - ط ١/ ١٤٢٢هـ

If the enemy deludes you to a point that the objectives and grounds of marriage are other than that which Allah ﷻ directed: {{there will be discord in the land and great corruption.}}

So, it is incumbent upon the mothers and fathers to place within their hearts this illuminated light of Prophetic rearing and the Illuminating light ﷺ spoke the truth upon saying: "Marry and beget children for I'll be proud before the nations on the Day of Resurrection."[8]

So, the boasting of the Chosen one ﷺ to the previous nations at the pond on Judgment Day is an aim for us, so does this cross the minds of the youth? Does this aim cross the minds of their fathers and mothers? Has the light of Prophetic rearing vanished from us and our thoughts as a result of influencing factors which have attacked us and invaded our homes and minds?

---

8 Reported by Abdul Razzaq in its weakness on the authority of Saeed bin Abi Hilaal, the narration is "*mursalan*", chapter of the obligation and virtue of marriage. (10391/173/6) "Al Majlis Al 'ilmi"-India–2 Ed. / 1403.

أي: إذا غركم الأعداء فصارت المقاصد في التزويجات والاعتبارات غير ما أرشد الله ﴿تَكُنْ فِتْنَةٌ فِي الْأَرْضِ وَفَسَادٌ كَبِيرٌ﴾

فلابد أن تضع الأمهات والآباء في قلوبهم نور هذه التربية النبوية، وصَدَقَ السراج المنير، حيث قال « تناكحوا تكثروا فإن مباءٍ بكم الأمم يوم القيامة »[8] فمفاخرة المصطفى للأمم السابقة على الحوض يوم القيامة مقصد لنا، فهل يخطر على بال الشاب والشابة هذا؟! وهل يخطر هذا المقصد على بال آبائهم وأمهاتهم!!؟ أم أن نور التربية النبوية انحجب عنا وعن أفكارنا بتأثيراتٍ داهمَتنا وداخلَتنا إلى بيوتنا وعقولنا؟!

_____

8   رواه عبد الرزاق في مصنفه عن سعيد بن أبي هلال مرسلاً ، باب وجوب النكاح وفضله (٦ /١٧٣/١٠٣٩١) المجلس العلمي - الهند - ط ٢ / ١٤٠٣

The Concern Toward the Raising of Children from the Beginning

There is a big responsibility upon the family related to the rais- ing of sons and daughters from the beginning which consists of:

1. Having the intention upon marriage.
2. Thereafter, during the pregnancy and being conscious of it.
3. Thereafter, upon birth and the infancy stage.
4. Thereafter, during the age of discretion.

All these stages which we are faced with, come with responsibil- ities and every stage has responsibilities which are specific to it that are greater and wider than the preceding stage.

Fulfilment of each obligation during a stage helps with passing to the next stage in a beautiful state, and every negligence during a stage from among these stages leads to difficulty in the proceeding stage and hardship toward the accomplishment of the affair.

الاهتمام بالتنشئة من البداية

على الأسرة مهمة كبيرة تتعلق بتنشئة الأبناء والبنات من بداية الأمر، ومعنى مِن بداية الأمر:

١ - من النية عند الزواج.

٢ - ثم من عند الحمل والشعور به.

٣ - ثم من عند الولادة وأيام الصبا.

٤ - ثم من عند سنِّ التمييز.

وكلها مراحل تتوجه علينا فيها مسؤوليات، ففي كل مرحلة مسؤوليات تخصها أكبر وأوسع من المرحلة السابقة.

وكلُّ أداءٍ للواجب في مرحلة يساعد على اجتياز المرحلة الثانية بحالٍ جميلٍ، وكلُّ تقصيرٍ في مرحلة من هذه المراحل يؤدي إلى تعبٍ في المرحلة التي بعدها وإلى مشقَّةٍ في القيام بالأمر.

First:
The Stage of Marriage

The first stage is the stage of marriage. It is necessary that it is performed with good intentions and understanding its purpose in life, such as what Allah ﷻ mentioned: {{And among His Signs, is that He created for you wives from among yourselves, that you may find tranquility in them and He has put affection and mercy between you. Verily, in that are indeed signs for a people who reflect.}} Surah Al-Rum, verse 21. Also, with that realization of that which the Prophet ﷺ mentioned: "… I will compete with the nations in superiority of numbers on Judgment Day."[9]

Allah ﷻ made mention of affection and mercy. Tranquility of the heart for the believers is established through mutual assistance in that which pleases Allah ﷻ, in the formation of a pious family and producing offspring who will come to the pond of Prophet Muhammad ﷺ on Judgment Day.

A sign of this:

A married couple does not to associate within their marriage that which contradicts the Sacred Law, not through ill speech nor offensive actions which are out of the limits of modesty.

---

9   Transmitted by Abu Dawood in his book *Sunan*, on the authority of Ma'ql bin Yasaar, chapter of prohibition of marrying an infertile woman. (2050/220/2) Al Maktbah Al Asriyyah, Sido –Beirut.

أولا: مرحلة الزواج

المرحلة الأولى مرحلة الزواج، فيجب أن يتمَّ بالنيَّاتِ الصالحات وبإدراك المهمة في الحياة.. ومنها ما ذكره الله عَزَّوَجَلَّ بقوله: ﴿وَمِنْ ءَايَتِهِ أَنْ خَلَقَ لَكُم مِّنْ أَنفُسِكُمْ أَزْوَاجًا لِتَسْكُنُوا إِلَيْهَا وَجَعَلَ بَيْنَكُم مَّوَدَّةً وَرَحْمَةً إِنَّ فِي ذَلِكَ لَآيَاتِ لِقَوْمٍ يَتَفَكَّرُونَ﴾ [الروم: ٢١]

ومنها تحقيق ما ذكره النبي ﷺ بقوله: (فإني مكاثرٌ بكم الأمم يوم القيامة) [٩] .

ذكر الله المودة والرحمة، وسكون قلب يقوم على التعاون على مرضاة الله تَعَالَى في تكوين أسرة صالحة في المؤمنين، يخرج منها نسلٌ يردون على الحوض المورود يوم القيامة على النبي محمد عَلَيْهِ الصَّلَاةُ وَالسَّلَامُ.

وعلامة ذلك: أن لا يصحب زواجَهم مخالفةٌ للشرع لا من الأقوال السيئة ولا من الحركات البشعة الخارجة عن الحياء.

---

[٩] أخرجه أبو داود في سننه عن معقل بن يسار ، باب النهي عن تزويج من لم يلد (٢٢٠/٢ /٢٠٥٠) المكتبة العصرية، صيدا - بيروت

For the marriage not to embrace the entering of a man in the company of strange women, and to not appear in front of them with his wife, whether he be holding her by the hand or closer, nor any other of these repulsive ungodly customs of the Christians and Jews. In fact from among the worst of Jews and Christians who are disreputable who act this way, there are from among them families which do not consent to this act for themselves nor their children, as a result of what remains within them from the natural disposition or traces of the previous prophets reaching them (may Allah's blessings and peace be upon them).

So how can a believing Muslim follow the worst of the Jews, Christians, and the sinful and lowest of disbelievers? Refuge is with Allah ﷻ!

At times there are hidden matters, which have entered upon families which then remove them from the illuminated and pure path. This was perhaps as a result of deception of something which the son and daughter were deceived through, but happily, boastfully, and proudly received it, while it takes away the most precious thing one possesses and removes one from the most honorable of positions and most dearest of ranks, and throws one into Hell. Despite the fact that one boasts and shows pride in it, happy with this ill and repulsive custom, it is contradictory to the Sacred Law, his religion, values, and pure legacy from his honorable predecessors. Refuge is with Allah ﷻ.

ولا يكتنف زواجَهم دخولُ الرجل على النساء الأجانب، ولا ظهوره أمامهن مع زوجته، لا آخذاً بيدها ولا ملقِّماً لها، ولا شيء من تلك العادات الكافرة الخبيثة الواردة من قِبَلِ النصارى واليهود، بل من شرار اليهود والنصارى، والساقطون منهم هم الذين يعملون هذا، فإن فيهم أُسَراً لا ترضى بهذا ولا تسمح لأولادها بفعلِ هذا، لما بقي عندهم من الفطرة أو مِن أثر ما كان مِن بلاغِ الأنبياء السابقين صلوات الله وسلامه عليهم.

فكيف يتَّبع المسلمُ المؤمنُ شِرارَ اليهود و النصارى وفسقة الكافرين المنحطين، والعياذ بالله تَبَارَكَ وَتَعَالَى!!!؟

فهنا دواخِل دخلت على الأُسَر أخرجتها عن المنهج الأنور الأطهر، وربما كان ذلك بخديعة خُدِع بها فتصير البنت ويصير الابن آخذًا لها بفرح وربما بافتخار واعتزاز، وهي تَسلب عليه أغلى شيء عنده، وتخرجه عن أكرم مكانة وأعز مرتبة، وترمي به إلى هاوية، وهو يفتخر ويعتز بها، فرحًا بهذه العادة الخبيثة السيئة المخالفة لشريعته، المخالفة لدينه المخالفة لقيمه المخالفة لتراثه الطيب من سلفه الأكرمين، والعياذ بالله تَبَارَكَ وَتَعَالَى.

Second:
The Stage of Pregnancy

Upon the realization of the pregnancy, one should perform the following:

An intention for the pregnancy, child, actions of the father and mother during the time of pregnancy, and the conversation between them which the unborn is made to hear from the words which arise from them. Also, the type of food which they consume and its goodness in terms of permissibility, purity, and physically beneficial as well as nutritional, because that which they consume from place to place has an effect on the fetus.

So, whatever it hears from its mother during the pregnancy and the sounds which it hears from the mother in or out the home, from that which is pure, Qur'ān, Remembrance and truth, all has an effect upon the fetus and is from among the group of influencing factors which builds the personality of this fetus, be it a boy or girl.

ثانيا: مرحلة الحمل

تأتي فيها عند إدراك الحمل: النية في الحمل، والنية في الولد، وأعمال الوالد والوالدة أيام الحمل، وما يسمعه من تحاورٍ بينهما، ومن كلمات تصدر منهما، ونوع الأكل الذي يأكلونه، وصلاحه من جهة الحِلِّ، ومن جهة الطُّهر، ومن جهة الفائدة الحسية والنوعية الغذائية أيضًا، فإن ما يتناولونه ويأكلونه من هنا ومن هناك مؤثرات وعوامل تؤثر على هذا الحمل.

فما يسمعه أيام الحمل من أمه، ومن الأصوات التي تسمعها أمه في البيت وخارج البيت، فاكان منها طيباً، وماكان منها قرآناً، وماكان منها ذكراً، وما كان منها صدقاً، مؤثِّرٌ على هذا الحمل، ومن جملة العوامل التي تبني شخصية هذا الحمل ابناً كان أو بنتاً.

Third:
The Stage of Birth

At this point, the obligations and responsibilities upon the mother and father toward the child increase significantly, after Allah ﷻ blows a soul into him; fashions his body completely with ears, eyes, skin, hair, flesh, blood and bones; and makes easy the path until he brings him out to the world. This then brings forth the role of establishment of the direction, good intentions, and actions connected to the Prophetic way which is firstly, after his exit and cutting of the umbilical cord:

1. To sound the call to prayer in the newborn's right ear and to sound the commencement of prayer in their left ear, which connects him to Allah ﷻ and His Messenger ﷺ from the beginning stages of his life.

2. To choose a good name for him and not that of a sinner, disbeliever, adulterer, and evil doer. In fact, they should consider the names of the prophets, companions, and pious folk to choose a good name for him, as this is among his rights upon them.

3. Thereafter they should perform the *Tahneek*, which is to be initiated with mentioning Allah's ﷻ name and remembrance of Him and His Messenger ﷺ. One should also request the pious and upright people to perform the *Tahneek* upon him, to gaze upon him, recite upon him, and make supplications for him. (*Tahneek* is the act of chewing and softening a little piece of date or any-

ثالثا: مرحلة الولادة

هنا تتكاثر وتتسع الواجبات والمهمات من الأب والأم نحو هذا الولد، بعد أن نفخ الله فيه الروح وكوَّنَ ذاك الجسد كاملًا بسمعِه وبصرِه وشعرِه ولحمه ودمِه وعظامِه، ويسَّرَ السبيلَ حتى أخرجه إلى عالم الأرض، هنا يأتي دور تقويم الوجهة، والنيات الصالحة والأعمال المرتبطة بالسنة التي من أولها بعد خروجه وقطع سُرِّدُ:

أن يؤذَّن في أذنه اليمنى، وتقام الصلاة في أذنه اليسرى، ربطاً له بالله ورسوله في أول مراحل عمره، وأن يُختار له الاسم الحسن لا اسم فاسق، ولا اسم كافر، ولا اسم فاجر، ولا اسم شرير.. بل ينظرون أسماء الأنبياء وأسماء الصحابة وأسماء الصالحين ويختارون له الاسم الحسن، وهو من حقوقه عليهم، ثم تحنيكُه، وفي تحنيكه تسمية الله، وذكرُه وذكرُ رسوله ﷺ، ثم طلب الصالحين والأخيار أن يحنِّكوه، وأن ينظروا إليه، وأن يقرؤوا عليه، وأن يدعوا له، فهذه مهمة من المهمات في أول النشأة.

ثم إرضاعه من الحلال، وتقديم لبن الأم على أي طعامٍ آخر، وأن لا ترضعه إلا باسم الله، وأن لا تشتغل أثناء رضاعه بتفرُّجٍ على مناظر سيئة، ولا بغيبةٍ

thing sweet and nutritious and thereafter placing it upon the baby's palate.)

So, these are from among the responsibilities at the beginning of birth.

Thereafter, he should be fed from that which is permissible, making the mother's milk a priority over any other food, and she should not feed him except with starting in the Name of Allah ﷾ and should not occupy herself during breastfeeding with looking at bad sights, nor engage in back biting or slander at home, but instead she should occupy herself, during the feeding, with the remembrance of Allah ﷾, recitation of the Qur'ān or any other good deed or speech which the newborn hears. This all has an effect on the newborn, just like we caused him to hear the Prophetic etiquette of the call to prayer in his ear at the beginning of his life without us expecting a response from him nor for him to stand up to perform prayer. However, so that we can fill his ear, heart, intellect, and mind with the name of Allah ﷾ and that of his Messenger ﷺ.

على أحد، ولا بنميمة في البيت تكلم بها ذا أو ذاك، ولكن تشتغل أثناء رضاعه بذكر الله، أو بتلاوة كتاب الله، أو بشيء من الخيرات والكلمات الطيبات التي يسمعها هذا الطفل، فإنها مؤثرات عليه كما سمعنا سُنِّيَةَ الأذان في أذنه، نُسْمِعُهُ الأذان وهو في بداية العمر لا ننتظر منه أن يجيب الأذان، ولا أن يقوم ليصلي!! ولكن لكي نحشوا أذنه ولبَّه وعقلَه وذهنَه باسم الله واسم رسوله عليه الصلاة والسلام .

Fourth:
The Stage of the Age of Discretion

At the beginning of the age of discretion, the affair upon them becomes greater and it is upon them to bring rise to within the child the correct understanding of Allah ﷻ, His greatness, His presence, and that He is the Creator of everything and has control over all things.

In fact, it is befitting that from the time they begin speaking for Allah's ﷻ name to be mentioned to him, in order for his tongue to become accustomed to the remembrance of Allah ﷻ and the mentioning of the name of Allah ﷻ and His Messenger ﷺ. So in this way, matters of rearing progress from the age of discretion with teaching him various etiquettes related to eating. Imam Ramli mentions in his poem about raising children:

> And after his weaning, you will notice his desire
> towards continuously and endlessly eating food
>
> So teach him to eat with the right [hand]
> and to always mention Allah's name [at the beginning]
>
> He should not leave before the completion of his companion
> ion
> and he should eat from the food which is nearest to him

رابعا: مرحلة التمييز

فإذا بدأ التمييز كان الأمر موجهاً بشكل أكبر عليهم أن يُنشِئوا عنده المعرفة الصحيحة بالله، وعظمة الله ووجود الله، وأنه خالق كل شيء، وبيده ملكوت كل شيء.

بل ينبغي من حين أن يبدأ بالنطق أن يُذكر له اسمُ الله، ليتعوَّد لسانُه ذكر الحق ﷻ، والنطق باسم الحق ورسوله محمد صلى الله عليه وآله وصحبه وسلم.

وهكذا تستمر شؤون هذه التربية من عند سن التمييز بأنواعٍ من تعليمه الآداب في أكله. قال الإمام الرملي في منظومة رياضة الصبيان:

وبعد فطمهِ تجده يشتهي

أكلَ الطعام دائماً لا ينتهي

فعلِّموه الأكلَ باليمين

والبسملة حتماً بكلِّ حين

ولا يبادرِ قبل أكلِ صاحبِه

ويأكل العيشَ الـذي بجانبه

He should properly chew his food
and he should not rush nor take more food [before chew-
    ing the current].

These are from among some of the etiquettes related to eating
and drinking in addition to these:

Teach the child to eat and drink with his right hand and start with
mentioning the name of Allah ﷻ, to not eat nor drink except while
sitting, to praise Allah ﷻ at the end of eating and drinking, to not
compete during it with others, and to not begin before someone who
is older than him.

For him to be taught the respect for elders from the beginning
of his upbringing and thereafter he prepares to enroll into a school.

ويمضغ اللقمة مضغاً محكمـا

ولا يسارع أو يوالي اللُّقَمَـا

وهكذا ما يتعلق بآداب الطعام والشراب ومنها: تعليمه الأكل باليمين والشرب باليمين، والبسملة، وأن لا يأكل إلا وهو قاعد، وكذلك أن لا يشرب إلا وهو قاعد، وأن يحمد الله بعد الطعام وبعد الشراب، ونعلِّمه أن لا يسابق غيره، ولا يتقدَّم على مَن هو أكبر منه.

ونعلِّمُه احترامَ من هو أكبر منه من بداية نشأته. ثم يتهيأ بعد ذلك للذهاب إلى المدرسة.

ʿFifth:
The Stage of School

When we prepare our son or daughter to enroll into a school, we should choose one which will not strip them of their character but rather increase them in light; one which combines knowledge and character and we should choose for them their male and female teachers.

When we choose for them a school which we see is good for them, then we have preserved our roles in terms of accountability to that which they study, memorize, and take in at school. So, the role of the mother is to check up on her daughter in school from time to time, inquiring about her state, uprightness, and acquisition of knowledge. In relation to that which she carries out at her home, she should ask her daughter what she has studied on that particular day, what she has read about, what homework she has, and what etiquettes she learned.

So this is an important role and if it is neglected, then much of the school's influence and benefit is lost from a girl, whose mother and father are not inquiring about what she is studying and learning. It may be that a whole academic year passes without them having come to her classroom, nor having inquired by the female principal about her, nor having inquired about her from the teachers who are teaching her, so it results in a type of negligence toward the affair of this girl and an inconsideration to her situation and state. So if this is also the case at home where they don't ask her, nor encourage her

خامسا: مرحلة المدرسة

فإذا تهيَّأ الابن أو البنت للذهاب للمدرسة اخترنا لهم المدرسة التي لا تسلُب عليهم أخلاقَهم، والتي تزيدهم نوراً، والتي تربط بين العلم والسلوك، واخترنا لهم المعلمين، واخترنا لهم المعلمات.

فإذا اخترنا لهم المدرسةَ التي رأينا فيها الخيرَ لهم، واصلنا أدوارَنا في مساءلتهم عما يدرسون وعما يتحفَّظون وعما يأخذونه في المدرسة. فمهمةُ الأم أن تتفقَّد بنتها في المدرسة، فتأتي الأم للمدرسة من وقتٍ لآخر تسأل عن حالة ابنتها وعن استقامتها وكيف استفادتها؟ مع ما تقوم به يومياً في بيتها من مساءلة البنت ماذا درستم اليوم؟ وماذا قرَأتم؟ وماذا عليك من الواجبات؟ وماذا تعلمت من الآداب؟

فذلك دورٌ مهم، وبإضاعته تضيعُ كثيرٌ من آثار المدرسة وفائدتها أمام هذه البنت التي لا تجد أماً ولا أباً يسألونها عماكان وعما تعلمت وعما تلقَّت، وربما مرّ العام الدراسي وما وصلوا يوماً إلى صفها الذي تدرس فيه، ولا سألوا عنها مديرة المدرسة، ولا سألوا عنها المدرسات اللاتي يُدرِّسنها، فيكون نوعٌ من الإهمال في شأن هذه البنت، وعدم مبالاةٍ بوضعِها وحالها، فإذاكان هذا مع

upon the memorization and writing of homework, what results then is a total negligence as far as the girl is concerned. Then the external influences start to have an effect on her from her female school mates and friends at school, who may be from among those who are rebellious and void of etiquettes, of which then flows toward this girl without her noticing nor the mother being aware of it.

It may be that they let her get taken by television programs which are void of piety, beauty, a correct direction in life, and belief in Allah ﷻ and His Messenger ﷺ, so she learns words, actions, perceptions, and thoughts from them which then has an effect on her personality and upbringing. The same applies for a boy.

أنهم في البيت أيضا لا يسألونها، ولا يشجعونها على المحفوظات الطيبة ولا على كتابة الواجبات، كان إهمالًا كاملًا في شأن هذه البنت، تبدأ تأثُّراتها حينئذٍ بمن حواليها من الصاحبات والصديقات وسط المدرسة، وقد يكون فيهن الشاذة أو المخالفة أو المضيّعة للآداب، فتبدأ سراية ذلك إلى هذه البنت، والأم في غفلة، والبنت أيضا في غفلة.

بل ربما سلَّموها بأنفسهم لتأخذَ زمامها برامجُ غير صالحة في التلفزيون و غير حسنة و غير قائمة على نظرة صحيحة في الحياة، وغير قائمة على إيمان بالله وبرسوله صلى الله عليه وآله وصحبه وسلم، فتعلمت منها كلماتٍ وأفعالًا ونظراتٍ وأفكاراً، فأثَّرت في شخصية هذه البنت وفي نشأة هذه البنت أو الابن كذلك.

An Address to the Legal Guardians

o not ignore, neglect or become careless toward these responsibilities, obligations, and roles relating to Allah's ﷻ
System of Successorship and one's direction in life. What then is your
responsibility?

What are your roles in life then if you were to neglect these obligations toward your sons and daughters at home, who are then given
to drink from the poison of the disbelievers, wrong doers, and sinful
from mankind and are disconnected in most of their dealings from
the light of revelation, Prophetic way, and guidance brought by Allah
ﷻ.

What is the value of a mother?

What is the role of a mother?

What is the value of a father?

What is the role of a father?

Wretched is the mother and father who give their children poison to drink and disconnect them from the protected Prophetic way
and the Divine lights of the Ever Living and Self Subsisting ﷻ.

These great and essential obligations of life are incumbent upon
us to carry them out as far as our sons, daughters, and other sib-
lings are concerned through mutual cooperation between husband
and wife, mother and father, maternal and paternal uncles, and big
brothers and sisters. This is in order for the completion of execution
of roles, cautioning and guiding, so we may preserve their character

نداء لأولياء الأمور

هذه مهمات وواجبات وأدوار في الخلافة عن الله، وفي المسار في الحياة لا تتغافلوا عنها ولا تهملوها، ولا تتساهلوا فيها، فما مهمتكم؟ وما دوركم في الحياة إذا أهملتم هذه الواجبات وسُقي الأبناءُ والبناتُ وسط دياركم مِن سمومِ الكفار والأشرار والفساق على ظهر الأرض، وانقطعوا في كثيرٍ من شؤون حياتهم عن نور الوحي، عن نورِ السنة، عن نورِ الهدى الذي جاءنا من الله تعالى.

فما قيمة الأم!؟

وما دور الأم!؟

وما قيمة الأب!؟

وما دور الأب!؟

بئست الأم وبئس الأب إذا سقَوا أولادَهم السموم، وقطعوهم عن سنة النبي المعصوم، وعن أنوار الحي القيوم جَلَّ وتعالى في علاه.

مهمات كبيرات أساسيات في الحياة يجب أن نقوم بها في شأن هؤلاء الأبناء

and protect them from the poison and vipers of the enemies of the Sacred Law, Religion, and upright character.

والبنات، يتعاون فيها الزوج مع الزوجة، والأم مع الأب مع الأعمام مع الأخوال مع الإخوان الكبار مع الأخوات الكبيرات، نتعاون بهم ومعهم على مَن بعدهم من إخوانهم الذين هم أصغر منهم، ليتكامل العطاء والأداء للدور والتنبيه والإرشاد، ولنحافظ على السلوك، ولنصونهم من سموم وأفاعي أعداء للشريعة وللدين وللسلوك القويم.

Mutual Cooperation Toward the Execution of the Role

At times, it may be that some mothers are negligent toward this role, so it is upon the fathers to encourage them toward this and likewise at times this negligence could come from the direction of the fathers toward their daughters, so it is likewise upon the mothers to encourage them toward this and to remind them in a clever and wise way that he has responsibilities other than food, drink, and clothing. So, they mutually assist each other in the rectification of their daughter's thinking, behavior, conduct, and connection toward her Lord, Prophet ﷺ, Hereafter, and religious mindset.

She should say to her husband: Let us raise a girl who will fulfill a good role in marriage and professional life, and this consists of her fulfilling the needs within the house and the family, in terms of what is required for the realization of tranquility and peace therein—Allah ﷻ mentions in His book: {{…that you may find tranquility in them…}} Surah Ar-Rum, verse 21.

So, this tranquility for the husband, sons, and daughters is attained through good assistance within the home and the fulfilling of the responsibilities therein.

So, she is prepared for this through the mutual cooperation of the mother and father toward this great responsibility, their mutual reminding of one another about their obligations and responsibilities, and carrying out of this responsibility which the best of creation

التعاون على أداء المهمة

قد يصادف بعضُ الرجال إهمالاً من الأم فيجب عليه أن يحرِّكَها في هذا المضمار، وأن يحرِّك فيها شعورَها. وقد تصادف بعض الأمهات أيضاً رجلاً يغفل عن مهمته نحو بنته، ويغفل عن مهمته نحو ولده وعن تربيتهم، فيجب عليها بعقلها وبحكمتها أن تحرِّك فيه ضميره، وتحرك فيه شعوره، وتحرِّك فيه إحساسَه، وتتذاكر معه في أن عليه مهمة غير الطعام والشراب واللباس.. فتتعاون معه على تقويم فكرِ البنت وسلوكها وأخلاقها وصلتها بربِّها وبنبيِّها وبآخرتها وبفكرِها الإيماني وتقول لزوجها: دعُنا نقيم بنتاً تؤدي دورها الطيب في الأسرة إذا انتقلت إلى الأسرة بعد الزواج، وفي مهمتها في الحياة إن ارتبطت بمهنة أو بحرفة أو بعمل أو أساسيات المهن والحرف، وهو أنها ربة بيت تقوم بحوائج البيت وما تحتاجه الأسرة وسط البيت بما يحقق السكينة والسكون الذي ذكره الله تعالى في كتابه ﴿لِتَسْكُنُوا إِلَيْهَا﴾ [الروم: ٢١]

فيكون ذلك السكون للزوج وللأبناء والبنات بحسن الخدمة وسط البيت والقيام بالمهمات هناك.

فنُعِدُّها لذلك بتعاون الأب والأم على هذه المهمة العظيمة، وتذاكرهم

ﷺ made mention of: "All of you are shepherds and each of you is responsible for his flock…"[10]

---

10   Transmitted by Al-Bukhari in his book *Sahih*, on the authority of Ibn Umar, chapter of a slave is responsible for the property of his master. (2409/120/3), Dar Tawq al-Najaah, 1st Ed. / 1422 AH.

لواجباتهم وتذاكرهم لمهماتهم وتذاكرهم للقيام بهذه المسؤولية التي قال عنها خير البرية ﷺ (ألا كلكم راع، وكلكم مسؤول عن رعيته). ١٠

١٠ أخرجه البخاري في صحيحه عن ابن عمر ، باب العبد راع في مال سيده (٢٤٠٩/١٢٠/٣) دار طوق النجاة - ط
١ - ١٤٢٢هـ

ʿExample of an Ideal Home

The home of Fatimah al-Zahra (May Allah be pleased with her) was an ideal, honorable, and noble example of a noble family which established within it Allah's ﷻ *System of Successorship*, so have you read the life story of Al-Zahra? Have you read how her father reared her while she was in the house of her mother, Khadijah, who passed away ten years after revelation had descended upon the Messenger ﷺ?

The Liege lady Fatimah was five years old when revelation descended, and then her mother passed away when she was fifteen, and thereafter she migrated at this age with her father to Madinah after the demise of her mother. For a period of three years at this time, she took up the role of serving her family including her father and sisters.

She completely took up the role of serving her father to the point that he used to call her "the mother of her father."[11]

The Messenger ﷺ used to say to her (May Allah be pleased with her): "O mother of her father."

She is a part of him who is distinguished with special attributes and traits.

She married our Master, Ali bin Abi Taalib, and started building a blessed family. She became established following the supplications

---

11 Transmitted by Al-Tabaraani in his book *Al Muʿjam Al-Kabir*, on the authority of Musʿab ibn Abdullah, chapter of the mentioning of the age of Fatimah (May Allah be pleased with her). (985/397/22), Maktabah Ibn Taymiyyah-Cairo-2nd Ed.

نموذج للبيت المثالي

كان بيت فاطمة الزهراء عليها رضوان الله ﷻ نموذجاً شريفاً كريماً للأسرة الكريمة في القيام بالخلافة عن الله تعالى، فهل قرأتم سيرة الزهراء؟ وهل قرأتم كيف رباها أبوها وهي في بيت أمها خديجة التي توفيت بعد أن نزل الوحي على رسول الله صلى الله عليه وآله وصحبه وسلم بعشر سنين.

كانت السيدة فاطمة في السنة الخامسة من عمرها حين نزل الوحي، ثم كانت وقت وفاة أمها في السنة الخامسة عشرة عليها رضوان الله ﷻ، ثم هاجرت في هذا السن إلى المدينة المنورة ووصلت إلى عند أبيها، وبعد وفاة أمها مكثت ثلاث سنين كانت القائمة بالدور وسط الأسرة وهي في هذا السن، وكانت تتولى خدمة أبيها، وخدمة أخواتها وسط البيت عليها رضوان الله ﷻ.

تولَّت الخدمة التامة لوالدها حتى سماها (أم أبيها)[11]، وكان يقول لها الرسول صلى الله عليه وآله وصحبه وسلم (يا أم أبيها) عليها رضوان الله ﷻ، وهي بضعة منه مخصوصة بخصائص ومزايا.

---

١١   أخرجه الطبراني في المعجم الكبير من حديث مصعب بن عبدالله، باب ذكر سن فاطمة ﵂ (٩٨٥/٣٩٧/٢٢) مكتبة ابن تيمية - القاهرة - ط ٢

from the Prophet ﷺ on her wedding night, and after carrying out a balance and middle path in terms of living standards, her father gave her an ablution item for the purpose of making ablution, a hand mill to grind corn, a leather mattress and cushion stuffed with palm fiber which he carried to the house which she had moved to, and further gifted her with gazes, supplications, directives, and invocations of protection. A blessed family was established on that night founded upon light and connected to the celestial realm.

In the second year of their marriage, Al-Hassan was born and thereafter Hussain, in the following year, followed by Zaynab, then Umm Kulthum. During his ﷺ lifetime, they grew up and received rearing from him in his noble home; he was the one who sounded the call and commencement to prayer in their ears and performed the *Tahneek* upon them with a date which he softened with his ﷺ noble saliva. He would take them along with him to the mosque up until his place of prayer, as well as his pulpit. He would frequent them and at times place them upon his back and shoulders and would play with them while rearing them.

He was the one that despite his love and rearing of them, when his grandson, Al-Hassan, ate one date from charity, he ﷺ came to him and instructed him to take it out from his mouth and placed his blessed finger there in and removed the date from the mouth of Al-Hassan, in order for him not to be soiled by the traces of a date unlawful to him. He ﷺ said: "(After instructing him to remove it from his mouth) Do you not know that we do not eat from charity?[12] Verily it is not lawful for Muhammad nor the family of Muhammad (and unhesitatingly removed it from his mouth.)"

---

12 Transmitted by Al-Bukhari in his book *Sahih*, on the authority of Abu Hurayrah, chapter of those who spoke Persian. (3072/74/4), Dar Tawq al-Najaah, 1st Ed. / 1422 AH.

وفي السنة الثانية من الهجرة تزوجت بعلي بن أبي طالب، وبدأ تكوين الأسرة المباركة، فقامت بعد دعوات من النبي في ليلة الزفاف، وبعد مظهر من الاعتدال والتوسط في أمر المعاش والمظاهر، زوَّدها أبوها ﷺ بمطهرة من أجل الوضوء، ورحى من أجل الطحن، وفراشٍ من جلد وحشوه من ليف، ووسادة حشوُها من ليف النخل، حملها إلى البيت الذي انتقلت إليه، وزوَّدها بالنظرات والدعوات والتوجهات والتحصينات، وقامت الأسرة المباركة في تلك الليلة على هذا النور والاتصال بالعالم الأعلى، وتكونت الأسرة.

وفي السنة الثانية من الزواج وُلِدَ الحسن، وفي السنة التي بعدها وُلِدَ الحسين، وتبعته زينب، ثم أم كلثوم في حياته ﷺ، وترعرعوا بين يديه وفي حِجره الكريم وربّاهم، وهو الذي أذَّن وأقام الصلاة في آذانهم، وحنَّكهم بالتمر الذي ليَّنه لهم بريقه الكريم، وكان يأخذهم معه إلى المسجد، ويستصحبهم إلى محرابه إلى منبره ﷺ، وكان يتردد عليهم، ويضعهم أحيانا على ظهره وعلى كتفه، وكان صلى الله عليه وآله وصحبه وسلم يلاعبهم ويربيهم.

وهو الذي مع محبته لهم وقيامه بتربيتهم لمَّا تناول ولده الحسن تمرةً واحدة من الصدقة جاء إليه وقال له: كِخْ كِخْ، وأدخل أصبعَه الكريم وأخرج التمرة من فم الحسن، حتى لا يتلطخ بأثر تمرةٍ لا تحلُّ له، وهو يقول: (كِخْ كِخْ، أَمَا تَعْرِفُ أَنَّا لَا نَأْكُلُ الصَّدَقَةَ)[12]، إنها لا تحل لمحمد ولا لآل محمد، وأخرجها من فمه صلى الله عليه وآله وصحبه وسلم، ولم يتردد في ذلك.

---

١٢ أخرجه البخاري في صحيحه عن أبي هريرة ، باب من تكلم بالفارسية (٣٠٧٢/٧٤/٤) دار طوق النجاة - ط ١ - ١٤٢٢هـ

He 鸞 would seek protection for them on a daily basis by saying: "I seek refuge for the both of you through the complete words
of Allah, from every devil and poisonous thing and from the evil
eye which influences." And he 鸞 would say: "Abraham, my father,
would seek the same protection for Ismail and Ishaq.[13] So I am seek-
ing protection for you through this." He 鸞 would teach them re-
membrances, good character, and principles.

He established them upon a noble structure in terms of rearing
through raising them upon etiquette, while being frequented by Angel Gabriel who would participate with him in gazing and rearing
of this upcoming generation. One day, Al-Hassan competed against
Hussein in wrestling; they were not aware of the Messenger 鸞 who
surprisingly started cheering Al-Hassan on, while our Liegelady
Fatimah was saying: "The bigger brother is being overcome by the
smaller!" He 鸞 addressed her and said "I did not say that except
that Angel Gabriel was on the opposing end cheering Hussein on, so
when Angel Gabriel did this, I stood beside this one[14], so that there
could be equality in the matter. So when they were still young, Angel
Gabriel would participate with them while they played.

In this rearing, how many a Divine Gaze and Assistance descended to form this blessed family!

Thereafter, Muhsin was born but died at a young age, leaving behind Zaynab and Umm Kulthum, who both had a big influence in
the history of this Ummah, the path of the pious, and the heirs of the
Prophet 鸞.

---

13   Transmitted by Ahmad in his *Musnad*, on the authority of Ibn Abbas, (2112/523/2) Dar ul
Hadith, Cairo-1st Ed. / 1416 AH (1995)

14   It was mentioned in the book of *Al Juawhar fi Nasab an Nabi wa As haabihi*, Author:
Muhammad Ibn Abi Bakr ibn Abdullah ibn Musa Al-Ansaari Al-Tilmasaani who was known as
Al-Burri (Died: After 645AH) Dar ul Rifaai' for publishing, printing and distribution, 1st ED./1402
AH (1984)

وكان يعوِّذُهما كل يوم فيقول للحسن والحسين: (أعيذكما بكلمات الله التامة من كل شيطان وهامّة، ومن كل عين لامّة»، وكان يقول: «كان إبراهيم أبي يعوِّذ بهما إسماعيل وإسحق)[١٣]، وإني أعوِّذُكُما بها. صلى الله عليه وآله وصحبه وسلم. وكان يعلمهما الأذكار، ويعلمهما المكارم والقيم.

أقامهم على تلك البنية الكريمة في التربية، ورباهم على تلك الآداب، وتردد عليه جبريل يشاركه في النظر إلى هؤلاء الناشئة وتربيتهم، ففي يوم من الأيام أخذ الحسن يتبارز مع الحسين ليصرع كل منهما صاحبه، ولم يعلموا إلا برسول الله صلى الله عليه وآله وصحبه وسلم يقول: إيهٍ يا حسن إيهٍ يا حسن فتقول له السيدة فاطمة: تغري الكبير بأخيه الصغير، قال لها ما قلت ذلك إلا وجبريل يقول إيهٍ يا حسين دونك الحسن، فلما قال جبريل كذا، وقفت أنا مع هذا)[١٤]، من أجل أن يتعادل الأمر، فيشاركهم في لعبتهم في الصغر جبريل أمين الوحي عليهم رضوان الله.

كم تنزّل في تلك التربية مِن نظرات الله وإمدادات الله، فتكونت تلك الأسرة المباركة. ثم ولد محسن ومات صغيرا، وبقيت بعده زينب وأم كلثوم، وكان لهما شأنٌ في تاريخ هذه الأمة، وفي مسلك الصالحين ووراثة سيد المرسلين

١٣ أخرجه أحمد في مسنده عن ابن عباس، مسند عبد الله بن عباس (٢/ ٥٢٣/ ٢١١٢) دار الحديث - القاهرة - ط ١/ ١٤١٦ هـ - ١٩٩٥ م

١٤ ذكره في كتاب الجوهرة في نسب النبي وأصحابه، تأليف: محمد بن أبي بكر بن عبد الله بن موسى الأنصاري التِّلِمْساني المعروف بالبَرِّي (المتوفى: بعد ٦٤٥هـ) دار الرفاعي للنشر والطباعة والتوزيع ط ١/ ١٤٠٣ هـ - ١٩٨٣ م

However, if minds are empty from imagining this goodness, to-gether with its mention and magnification while being filled with in-formation of abased and disreputable actresses, how will the rearing be? How will the role be? How will our children be reared? How will our daughters be reared?

صلى الله عليه وآله وصحبه وسلم. ولكن إن كانت الأذهانُ خاليةً عن تصوُّر هذه الخيرات وذكرِها وإعظامها، وحُشيت بأخبار الممثلات الساقطات الهابطات، فكيف تكون التربية؟ وكيف يكون الدور؟ وكيف نربي الأبناء؟ وكيف نربي البنات؟

Lessons Which Al-Hassan Benefited from the Messenger of Allah ﷺ

Al-Hassan said, after the demise of his grandfather, when he was eight years old: "One of the sayings of the previous prophets, which has been conveyed to the people is: 'If you have no modesty, then you can do whatever you like.'"[15]

So, he learned from him ﷺ modesty and good character during this early age, as his grandfather would cast toward him these teachings and reminders about these traits, good character, and meanings.

He also said: "I memorized from the Prophet ﷺ the saying of: "Leave that which is doubtful for you, for that which is not doubtful for you."[16] This means:

Distance yourself from suspicious matters, areas of heedlessness and hazard, and make the most cautious of decisions. Distance yourself from that which is doubtful and that which will cause you to enter into a state of doubt and suspicion, for that which is clear, evident, and free from suspicion and doubt. Upon this was the rearing from the Messenger ﷺ.

---

15 Transmitted by Ahmad in his *Musnad*, on the authority of 'Uqbah ibn 'Urwah, Chapter of the remaining Hadith of Abi Masuud, (17098/325/28) Muasistah al-Risalah, 1st Ed./1421 AH (2001)

16 Transmitted by Ahmad in his *Musnad*, on the authority of Al-Hawra al-Sa'di and Hasan ibn Ali, Chapter of the Hadith of Hasan ibn Ali, (1723/249/3) Muasistah al-Risalah, 1st Ed./1421 AH (2001)

دروس استفادها الحسن من رسول الله

قال الحسن وقد توفي جده وهو في الثامنة من العمر عليه رضوان الله: حفظت من رسول الله صلى الله عليه وآله وصحبه وسلم أنه قال: (إن ما أدرك الناسُ من كلام النبوة الأولى إذا لم تستحِ فاصنع ما شئت)[15]. تعلم منه شأن الحياء، وتعلم منه شأن الخلق الكريم وهو في هذا السن المبكر، وكان يلقي إليه جدُّه هذه التعاليم وهذه التنبيهات على هذه القيم وهذه الأخلاق والمعاني.

ويقول أيضاً: حفظت من النبي صلى الله عليه وآله وصحبه وسلم قول (دع ما يريبك إلى ما لا يريبك)[16] أي: ابتعد عن الشبهات وابتعد عن مواطن الغِرَّة ومواطن التَّجرِّئ، وخُذ بالأحوط، وابعِد عما يريبك وعما يداخلك من الشك والريب إلى أمرٍ واضح بيِّن لا ريب فيه ولا شك، فكذلك ربّاه صلى الله عليه وآله وصحبه وسلم.

---

١٥ أخرجه أحمد في مسنده عن عقبة بن عمرو، باب بقية حديث أبي مسعود (٢٨/ ٣٢٥/ ١٧٠٩٨) مؤسسة الرسالة - ط ١/ ١٤٢١ هـ - ٢٠٠١ م

١٦ أخرجه أحمد في مسنده عن الحوراء السعدي عن الحسن بن علي، باب حديث الحسن بن علي (١٧٢٣/٢٤٩/٣) مؤسسة الرسالة - ط ١/ ١٤٢١ هـ - ٢٠٠١

Mutual Assistance Between the Home and the School

We should be aware and take a glance at these responsibilities and collectively assist each other in establishing them, so the school has a role that if it were that the fathers and mothers embraced, it would become complete and prepare the upcoming generation to be pious individuals within the community and pure members from whom goodness is derived. They would also be a benefit to their time, community, country, life, and age within the Nation.

However, if the family does not carry out this role then neither the daughter nor son will benefit from the school, even if it were upon a good path. What then if that same school was deficient in its rearing and negligent toward the establishment of its obligation?

So, it's necessary that the measure of rearing be the same which the Prophet ﷺ, his companions, his household, and the families were upon who lived in his honorable and blessed community.

By the praise of Allah ﷻ, we find within some schools, a concern toward Prophetic invocations such as that of eating, drinking, and waking up from sleep. If this is combined with a pure and pious family concerned with them, it will result in these etiquettes becoming established. There is also a concern toward the girls' and boys' uniform, which is connected to the Prophetic way and guidance.

So, preserve this O mother and do not change the Mastership of Muhammad ﷺ and his daughter Al-Zahra, for that of the sinful, abased, and disreputable actresses who appear in various programs.

التعاون بين البيت والمدرسة

هذه مهماتٌ يجب علينا أن ننتبه منها وننظر إليها ونتساعد على القيام بها، فالمدرسة لها دور إن اكتنفه توجُّه الآباء والأمهات تمَّ الدور وكمُل، وتهيأ الناشئة لأن يكونوا أفراداً صالحين في المجتمع، وعناصر طيبة يُستقى منها الخير، نافعة في زمنها وفي مجتمعها وبلدها وفي حياتها وعمرها في الأمة.. وإن لم تؤدِّ الأسرةُ الدورَ لم يستفد الابن ولا البنت من المدرسة وإن كانت على مسار حسن، فكيف إذا كان في المدرسة نفسها خللٌ في التربية!! وإهمالٌ في القيام بالواجب. فلا بد أن يكون ميزان التربية على ما كان يربي عليه النبي صلى الله عليه وآله وصحبه وسلم أصحابَه وأهلَ بيته والأسر الذين عاشوا في مجتمعه الشريف المبارك صلى الله عليه وآله وصحبه وسلم.

وبحمد الله تعالى نجد في بعض المدارس اهتماما بالأذكار النبوية، فيتعلمون أذكاراً للأكل، وللشرب، وللقيام للنوم، وإذا وجدوا أسرة طيبة صالحة راعوهم في ذلك قامت هذه الآداب. ووجدنا كذلك اللباس الذي رُتِّب للبنات والبنين متصلا بالسنة متصلا بالهدي النبوي، فحافظي عليه يا أم، ولا تحوِّلي أستاذية محمد صلى الله عليه وآله وصحبه وسلم وابنته الزهراء بأستاذية الفاسقات الساقطات الهابطات الممثلات ومن يظهرن في البرامج المختلفة..

Our Master and Prophet is Muhammad ﷺ, so preserve this.

It's befitting for the sons to be vigilant upon the Prophetic dress code and I mean by that, a dress which is the most beloved to the Messenger ﷺ.

It's necessary that the dresses of the girls be completely concealing, wide and not tight, long and loose-fitting, and not short. It's necessary that we teach shyness and modesty from childhood and youth, so it's upon the family to take note of this affair and likewise it's upon the headmistress and school to pay attention to the dress code of the girls. However, when the girl grows up and concealment becomes necessary, then the affair becomes bigger, greater, and more dangerous, as she is not allowed to reveal any part of her beauty or body in the street, going or coming from school. Her inner garment which she wears in the company of women and at schools should be modest.

أستاذنا نبينا محمد صلى الله عليه وآله وصحبه وسلم، فحافظي على هذا..

وينبغي على البنين أن يحرصوا على لباس السنة، وأقصد به القميص الذي كان أحب اللباس إلى رسول الله صلى الله عليه وآله وصحبه وسلم.

ولا بد أن يكون لباس البنات ساتراً كاملاً، فضفاضاً لا ضيقاً، ويكون سابغاً لا قصيراً، فينبغي أن نتعلم الحياء والحشمة من الصبا ومن الصغر ونعلمهن ذلك. فعلى الأسرة أن تلاحظ هذا الأمر. كما أنه من واجب المديرة وواجب المدرسة أن تلاحظ أيضاً أزياء البنات اللاتي يحضرن، أما إذا بدأت البنت تكبر ووجب عليها الستر فالشأن أكبر وأعظم وأخطر، فلا يجوز أن تبدي شيئاً من زينتها، ولا أن تُظهِر شيئاً من جسدها في الشارع وأثناء خروجها إلى المدرسة ولا أثناء رجوعها، ويكون لباسها الداخلي الذي يكون عند النساء وفي المدرسة لباس حشمة ولباس حياء.

Rearing Upon Shyness, Modesty, and Concealment

The Qur'ānic and Prophetic rearing had an effect on our predecessors and those that came before us up until our youths' time.
When we came to know of them, here in the this city of Tarim to the
extent that the hair of a maiden girl would not be known by her sisters, aunties, and female relatives. Out of concealment and modesty
she would remove her hair herself and not get into a situation where
she should reveal her hair. However, starting a few years ago up until
now (the time of our youth), we have heard of the transgression of
the limits regarding this, that young girls from among our maiden
girls are brought to places of married women to sing for them while
not being concealed in their dress code and engage in movements
similar to that of the abased women!

Who are we following? Who is planning for us? Who is our role
model? And where are they taking us? Allah ﷻ says: {{And do
not marry polytheistic women until they believe. A believing slave
woman is better than a polytheist, even though she might please
you. Do not marry polytheistic men [to your women] until they believe. A believing slave is better than a polytheist, even though he
might please you. Those invite [you] to the Fire, but Allah invites
to Paradise and to forgiveness, by His permission. He makes clear
His verses to the people that perhaps they may remember.}} Surah
Al-Baqarah, verse 221.

التربية على الحياء والحشمة والستر

لقد أثرت التربية القرآنية المحمدية في سلفنا وماضينا إلى العصر الذي أدركناه في صِغرنا في هذه البلدة - تريم - فماكان يَعرِفُ شَعَرَ البنت العذراء أخواتُها، ولا عماتها ولا خالاتها بل قريباتٌ منها لا يعرفن ذلك، حرصاً منها على الستر والحياء، تزاول شعرها بنفسها، ولا تعرض نفسها لإظهار شيءٍ من شعرها. ومن سنوات قليلة من أيام صغرنا إلى الآن سمعنا عن تخطي الحدود في هذا الجانب، وأن بناتاً من بناتنا العذارى يدخلن إلى أماكن الزواجات ويقدمن الأغاني وهن متكشفات، ويتحركن بالحركات الساقطات!!

وراء مَن نمشي، ومن يخطط لنا، وبمَن نقتدي، وإلى أين يذهبون بنا؟

يقول الله ﷻ ﴿وَلَا تَنكِحُوا الْمُشْرِكَاتِ حَتَّى يُؤْمِنَّ وَلَامَهُ مُؤْمِنَةٌ خَيْرٌ مِّن مُّشْرِكَةٍ وَلَوْ أَعْجَبَتْكُمْ وَلَا تُنكِحُوا الْمُشْرِكِينَ حَتَّى يُؤْمِنُوا وَلَعَبْدٌ مُّؤْمِنٌ خَيْرٌ مِّن مُّشْرِكٍ وَلَوْ أَعْجَبَكُمْ أُولَئِكَ يَدْعُونَ إِلَى النَّارِ وَاللَّهُ يَدْعُو إِلَى الْجَنَّةِ وَالْمَغْفِرَةِ بِإِذْنِهِ، وَيُبَيِّنُ آيَاتِهِ لِلنَّاسِ لَعَلَّهُمْ يَتَذَكَّرُونَ﴾ [البقرة: ٢٢١]

Allah ﷻ says: {{...and if you obey most of those upon the earth, they will mislead you from the way of Allah. They follow not except assumption, and they are not but falsifying.}} Surah Al-An'aam, verse 116.

So be attentive upon her departure to school and upon every departure, even if she departs to somewhere else other than school, such as the house of her relatives or any occasion. Pay attention as to how she departs; pay attention to her at home; and don't let yourself become a victim of receiving clothes made from the hands of repulsive plotters who will then expose our daughters, teach them immodesty, and rear them upon unveiling.

Some women may say as an excuse to their leniency in this affair: This clothing is permissible!

Is it permissible as far as your Lord and Prophet Muhammad ﷺ are concerned?

This thobe is permissible for a satanic and sinful Jew who made this for you in a repulsive factory and you say that the clothing is permissible! Did Allah ﷻ make you a female slave to them so that you should follow them? Sew your own clothes and if you don't know how to sew, then complete the deficiency therein, so that it may appear appropriate to the religion, modesty, decency, rearing, Allah's ﷻ *System of Successorship* upon his land, Qur'ān, Prophetic way, and the way of the pious predecessors (may Allah ﷻ be pleased with them all). How did we turn the scales in just a few years until we descended and fell extensively? We seek refuge in Allah! So, may Allah ﷻ preserve for us our realities of faith and religion and grant us the ability to mutually cooperate upon that which is pleasing to Him.

ويقول جَلَّ ﴿وَإِن تُطِعْ أَكْثَرَ مَن فِي الْأَرْضِ يُضِلُّوكَ عَن سَبِيلِ اللهِ إِن يَتَّبِعُونَ إِلَّا الظَّنَّ وَإِنْ هُمْ إِلَّا يَخْرُصُونَ﴾ [الأنعام: ١١٦]

فلاحظي عند خروجها للمدرسة وعند كل خروج، وإن خرجت لغير المدرسة، وإن ذهبت لبيت أقاربها، وإن ذهبت لأي مناسبة أنظري كيف تخرج، لباسها وسط البيت لاحظيه، وانظري إليه، ولا تكوني عرضةً لأزياء تأتي إلينا صنعتها أيادي ماكرة خبيثة لتكشِّف بناتنا، ولتعلمهن قِلَّ الحياء، وتربيهن على السفور..

تقول بعض النساء محتجةً على التساهل في هذا الأمر: هذا ثوب جاهز! هل هو جاهز من عند ربك أو من عند النبي محمد؟!

هذا الثوب جاهز من مصنع خبيث فاسق وشيطان يهودي صنع لك هذا، وقلت جاء الثوب جاهزًا!! وهل خلقك الله أمةً له تتبعينه!؟ خيطي لك ثيابك، وإن لم تعرفي الخياطة أكملي ما نقص فيه حتى يظهر بمظهر يتناسب مع الدين ومع الحياء ومع الحشمة ومع التربية ومع الخلافة عن الله في أرضه ومع القرآن ومع ومع هدي السلف الصالحين عليهم رضوان الله ﷾، فكيف في سنوات قليلة قلَّبنا الموازين، فنزلنا هذا النزول وسقطنا هذا السقوط المهين والعياذ بالله تعالى!! فالله يحفظ علينا حقائق إيماننا وديننا، ويرزقنا التعاون على مرضاته.

Supplementary Matters of Rearing

Once we are aware of these basics and obligations, these are followed by supplementary matters among them:

Early attendance to school and the assembly to benefit from listening to verses from the Qur'ān and Hadith, as well as participating in their presentation, as the father and mother are pleased by their son or daughter's participation in the assembly and their presentation to the congregation of a verse from the Qur'ān, Hadith, advice, poetry or wise words from one of the pious. Therein is goodness leading toward guidance and liberation from evil and corruption, so they can be affected by goodness and become teachers in the future.

So likewise, should be the mutual cooperation among parents toward their children, so that they become successful and distinguished individuals who soundly carry out their roles at school.

كماليات

إذا انتهينا من هذه الأساسيات والواجبات تأتي بعد ذلك كمالياتٌ في التربية، ومنها:

الحضور المبكر للمدرسة والمجيء لحضور الطابور، والاستفادة من سماع الآيات والأحاديث، والمشاركة في التقديم، فإن الأب والأم يفرحان إذا شارك الابن أو البنت في الطابور وتلوا آياتٍ من القرآن، أو قدموا حديثاً، أو ذكروا نصيحة، أو قرأوا أبياتاً أو حِكَماً لأحد الصالحين على أهل الجمع بالطابور، فيها تبيين للخير وإرشاد للهدى وفيها تحرير من الشر والفساد ليكونوا مؤثرين في الخير ومعلمين للناس في مستقبلهم.

هكذا يجب أن يكون تعاون الأبوين مع أولادهم ليكونوا مميَّزين فائزين قائمين بأدوار طيبة في المدرسة.

Methodologies of Rearing and Their Means of Implementation

From many of that which is spoken about regarding rearing in today's time or methodologies, partial success is witnessed therein, so we say: Our objective of rearing is not short sighted nor limited to this life, but the objective of rearing is a complete outlook which recognizes the concern toward benefactors for this human being outwardly, inwardly, in this life, and in the hereafter and beyond in his eternal and permanent life which is without an ending nor limit.

These methodologies could lead some minds to realize short sighted and transitory goals or a realization of great eternal goals. The methodologies could involve a combination of both; however, it's not permitted for it to slip into the minds of a believer that following these methodologies requires a disconnection from the Protected Sacred Law and Divine Directives. In fact, we say: "If benefiting from experiences and taking means to reach goals and objectives and allows one to arrive there while others have had successful experiences with only this temporal life due to short sighted goals, then our implementation of these should be to derive benefit for both worlds and to serve elevated objectives. Our usage and acting upon them is free from that which pierces our connection and relation to this Protected Sacred Law and is not through directives from other than the Sacred Law itself. Some intellects have become deceived and some minds and souls have been captured by that adornment which has

الوسائل وطرق التعامل معها في قضية التربية

كثيرا ما يُتحدَّث به عن التربية في واقع هذه الحياة من أساليب أو وسائل، قد يُشاهدُ لها نجاحاً في الوصول إلى غرض ما، فنقول: ليس المقصود لنا بالتربية النظر القاصر ولا المحدود على الحياة الدنيوية، ولكن المقصود بالتربية النظر المتكامل الذي يعرف مراعاة المصلحة لهذا الإنسان في ظاهره وباطنه ودنياه وآخرته وما بعد مماته، في حياةٍ أبده وخلوده التي لا نهاية لها ولا انقضاء ولا فناء ولا غاية.

إن هذهِ الوسائلَ قد تهتدي إليها العقول لتحقيق أغراضٍ قصيرةٍ أو فانية، أو تحقيق أغراض عظيمة أبدية، قد تتحد الوسائل، ولكن لا يجوز أن يتسرَّبَ إلى عقل المؤمن أن الاهتداء إلى هذه الوسائل يكون بانقطاعٍ عن الشرع المصون وعن توجيهات الرب، بل نقول: إن الاستفادة من التجارب والأخذ بالوسائل للوصول إلى الأغراض والمقاصد، إن توصل بها الغير وجرَّبها في النجاح في حياتهم القصيرة وأغراضهم القريبة فإن استعمالنا لها للوصول من خلالها إلى مصلحة الحياتين وخدمة المقاصد السامية العليا، وأخذَنا لها وعَمَلَنا بها منزهةً عما يقدح في ارتباطنا وانتمائنا لهذا الشرع المصون ليس إلا من توجيه الشرع نفسه، لا يعود ولا ترجع فيها الخيرية ولا النجاح إلى كفر ولا إلى انقطاع عن الشرع، كما تُخدع بعض العقول وتؤسر بعض الأفكار والنفوس

appeared to people in this life. They are in pursuit of it during the days in which they should be preparing for purity and the uncovering of the light of revelation of the Supreme Owner, such as the splendored days of Ramadan. However, at times, these desires of the agents which cause one to be distanced may densify preventing the comprehension of the realities and cause a people of high principles and objectives to become debased. An increase and spread of such agents could cause one to become in a state of delusion and in fact, a state of misguidance, causing the level of thought to descend away from the illumination of the light of the Truth ﷻ via the Qur'ānic lights; the Clear light and his message ﷺ; and that which those after him from among his helpers, successors, and supporters carried.

بذلك الزخرف الذي يبثُّ للناس في هذه الحياة، والذي ربما طاردوا به الناس حتى في الأيام التي يستعدون فيها للصفاء، وانكشاف نور الوحي للملك الأعلى، كأيام رمضان الزهية، فقد تتكثفُ إرادات هذه المبعِدات عَن إدراك الحقائق لتهوي بأهل القيم والمقاصد السامية فتتكاثر عليهم وتنتشر بينهم في مثل هذه الليالي ما يوقع في تأكيد الوهم والخيال، بل والضلال، وما يُنزل مستوى الفكر عن الاستضاءة بنور الحق ﷻ من خلال سُرج قرآنه والسراج المبين وبيانه، وما حمله من النور مَن بعده من أنصاره وخلفائه وأعوانه صلى الله عليه وعلى آله وصحبه وسلم .

Conclusion and Final Remarks

O believing women, your roles in life are great and important. May Allah 𝕵 assist you all in its fulfillment, mutual reminding, and studying. Allah 𝕵 says: {{By Time, verily man is at loss, except those that have faith, do righteous deeds and (join together) in the mutual teaching of truth and patience.}} Surah Al-Asr, verses 1-3.

So be upon this manner during your mutual reminding and bring to heart your obligation. Assist the school so that the teaching and performance of the teachers may improve as well as the houses and families, which will result in us becoming more beautiful, elevated, God fearing, lasting, and purer by the will of Allah 𝕵 . This is attained through mutual cooperation among us, our schools, gatherings, homes, families, fathers, mothers, teachers, headmistresses, and scholars within the community. Through this we form a sound path for us in life from that which is beloved to our Giver of life, Who is the One that causes us to die and to Him is our final destination. He is our Supporter and Aide and upon Him is our reliance and dependence. Our Lord, the Most Compassionate, the Most Merciful, Who no one has participated in our creation besides Him, so therefore no one will participate besides Him in our rectification or direction. Not the people of the east nor west. In fact, we are the slaves of Allah 𝕵, the One, the Indivisible, the Ever living, the Subsisting. O Allah, the One who grants the ability for the people of goodness to

خاتمة وتوصيات

أيتها المؤمنات أدواركن في الحياة كبيرة ومهمة، أعانكن الله على القيام بها، تذاكرن وتدارسن فيها، قال تعالى: ﴿وَالْعَصْرِ إِنَّ الْإِنْسَانَ لَفِي خُسْرٍ إِلَّا الَّذِينَ ءَامَنُوا وَعَمِلُوا الصَّالِحَاتِ وَتَوَاصَوْا بِالْحَقِّ وَتَوَاصَوْا بِالصَّبْرِ﴾ [العصر: ٣ - ١]

فكنَّ على هذا المنوال في تذاكركن واستشعار واجبكن، وتعاوَنَّ مع المدرسة لتكون الدراسة، وأداء المدرسات أفضل، وكذلك البيوت والأسر لنكون كلنا أحسن وأرقى وأفضل وأتقى وأبقى وأنقى إن شاء الله، وإنما يحصل ذلك بالتعاون فيما بيننا، وبين مدارسنا وبين مجالسنا في ديارنا وأسرنا، وبين الآباء والأمهات، وبين المدرسات والمديرات، وبين علمائنا في المجتمع، بذلك نكوّن صحة مسارنا في الحياة على ما أحبه منا محُيينا والذي هو يميتنا وإليه مصيرنا، وهو نصيرُنا وعونُنا وعليه توكُّلنا واعتمادنا، ربنا الرحمن الرحيم الذي لم يشاركه في خلقنا أحد، فلا يشاركه في استقامتنا ولا في توجُّهنا أحد من أهل الشرق ولا من أهل الغرب، بل نحن عباد الله الواحد الأحد الحي القيوم، اللّهم يا من وفّق أهل الخير للخير وأعْنهم عليه وفقنا للخير وأعنا عليه.

بارك الله في الأمهات وفي بناتهن وأبنائهن مباركة تامة، اللّهم اجعلهن صالحات

perform goodness and assists them thereupon, grant us the ability to do goodness and assist us thereupon.

May Allah ﷻ extensively and completely bless the mothers together with their sons and daughters. O Allah, make them from among the righteous women who are devoutly obedient, guarding in absence what Allah would have them guard. O Ever living, O Subsisting, grant them firmness upon that which You love from speech, actions, objectives, and intentions. Grant them felicity in their families, communities, and lives in a state of goodness and make death peaceful from all evil, for us and them.

O Allah, rectify all our affairs the way You rectified the affairs of the pious, and cause us to die upon goodness and certainty. Grant us protection in our way of life and progress, and path upon the way of the upright, God-fearing people of goodness, and protect us from imitating the disbelievers and immoral. Allow us to attain our hopes and wishes in this life, the intermediary life, and the Hereafter. Grant us felicity in all our affairs, such as that felicity You granted those special people of felicity, inwardly and outwardly. May Peace and abundant blessings be upon our Master Muhammad, his family, and companions. All praise is due to Allah ﷻ.

قانتات حافظات للغيب بما حفظتَ يا حي يا قيوم ثبتهنَّ على ما تحب في الأقوال والأفعال والمقاصد والنيات وأسعدِهن في أسرهن وفي مجتمعهن وفي حياتهن حيازةً لهن لكل خير، واجعل الموت راحةً لنا ولهن من كل شر.

اللّهم أصلح لنا شأننا كله بما أصلحتَ به شأنَ الصالحين، واختم لنا بالحسنى واليقين، وارزقنا حفظ السيرة وحفظ المشي والمسار، في مسلك الأبرار الأتقياء الأخيار وأعِذنا من التشبه بالكفار والفجار، وبلِّغنا الآمال والأوطار في الدنيا والبرزخ والآخرة، وأسعِدنا بما أسعدتَ به خواص السعداء في جميع الشؤون ظاهراً وباطناً. وصلى الله على سيدنا محمد وآله وصحبه وسلم، والحمد لله رب العالمين.

www.ingramcontent.com/pod-product-compliance
Lightning Source LLC
Chambersburg PA
CBHW030852090426
42737CB00009B/1200